# HOPE AGAIN

### A LIFETIME PLAN FOR CONQUERING DEPRESSION

MARK SUTTON
BRUCE HENNIGAN, M.D.

*From Bruce:*
*I dedicate this book to the one person who has seen me through the darkest days of my depression and has consistently encouraged and loved me, my wife, Sherry. Her steadfast and unfailing love through times of difficulty and stress have always been my rock and my foundation. And, her devotion to our Lord and Savior has always been OUR rock and OUR foundation!*

*From Mark:*
*To Donna, my wife, best friend, spiritual partner: thank you for unconditional love, the gift of laughter, and beaming constant sunshine into my life. I have come alive because of you.*

Copyright © 2019 by Mark Sutton and Bruce Hennigan All rights reserved. Printed in the United States of America

Published by Hope Again Books
An Imprint of LifeFilters, LLC

Unless otherwise noted, Scripture quotations are from the Holy Bible, New International Version, © 1973, 1978, 1984 by International Bible Society.

Also used New King James Version (NKJV) © 1979, 1980, 1982, Thomas Nelson, Inc., Publishers; New Revised Standard Version (NRSV), © 1989 by the Division of Christian Education of the National Council of Churches of Christ in the United States of America, used by permission, all rights reserved; God's Word (CW), GOD'S WORD', © 1995 God's Word to the Nations. Used by permission of Baker Publishing Group; English Standard Version (ESV), copyright © 2001 by Crossway, a publishing ministry of Good News Publishers. ESV Text Edition: 201; Holman Christian Standard Bible (HCSB), Copyright © 1999, 2000, 2002, 2003, 2009 by Holman Bible Publishers. Used by permission; The Message (The Message), the New Testament in Contemporary English, © 1993 by Eugene H. Peterson, published by NavPress, Colorado Springs, Colo.; Contemporary English Version (CEV), © American Bible Society 1991, 1992; used by permission; New Living Translation (NLT), copyright 1996, 2004. Used by permission of Tyndale House Publishers, Inc., Wheaten, Illinois. All rights reserved; New Century Version (NCV), copyright © 2005 by Thomas Nelson, Inc. Used by permission. All rights reserved.

Book Cover Design by ebooklaunch.com

Logo design by http://www.juanjpadron.com

Cover Photograph by Bruce Hennigan — Good Shepherd Church on the South Island of New Zealand.

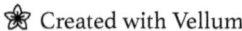 Created with Vellum

# LIFEFILTERS

Throughout this book, we emphasize the use of LifeFilters. What is a LifeFilter? As you work through the chapters/days you will discover the usefulness of our LifeFilter. There is a LifeFilter for each day coupled with a Bible verse. We suggest you write down that day's LifeFilter on a card and perhaps laminate that card to use on a daily basis. Carry your LifeFilter with you throughout the day to remind you of the important points you learned in that day's chapter. After the first thirty days, go through the LifeFilters again one day at a time.

You do not have to create your own LifeFilters. We offer laminated, preprinted LifeFilters on our website, www.conqueringdepression.com. You can order a set and we will ship it to you promptly.

Whatever form you choose for your LifeFilters, realize they are indispensable and will provide a powerful daily tool in conquering depression!

Bruce Hennigan

# SECTION ONE
## "WHAT'S WRONG WITH ME"

I (Mark) had a normal, happy childhood, something I now realize many adults cannot claim. My parents were Christians, actively living out the Christian life. They had a great marriage, and though we were what would today be called "lower middle class," I never really knew it. I was, and still am, the class clown, the kid who is good-natured and sees the humor in everything.

In my nineteenth year, however, something happened. A darkness fell over my life. It went on for months, and I couldn't shake it, no matter how I tried. My energy plummeted; my grades suffered; all I wanted to do was stay in my dorm room with the lights off. Normally a very social person, I now craved being alone. Tortured by negative thoughts and guilt that I couldn't even name, I remember often saying, "*What's wrong with me?*"

Perhaps you can identify. I now know that, for whatever reason, depression had descended upon my life. It has remained there ever since. HOWEVER, (and that's a big "however"), though it took me about fifteen years to figure out what was happening to me, I now have a battle plan.

I *know* what is happening to me, and it doesn't scare me anymore. I have a plan that I put into practice daily, no matter what my emotional outlook, *and it works!* So does Bruce. In other words, we practice what we preach. Through the grace of God, and through the strength of Christ who indwells us, we have conquered depression!

Now turn to Day One and begin your journey out of the darkness and into the light. Learn what's wrong, and discover the plan that will conquer depression.

# 1

## DAY ONE

# THE POWER TO CONQUER

Let's begin with lobsters.

Yes, you read that right. You'll understand my point in just a moment. Because lobsters are territorial, they take any incursion into their area quite seriously. Often, both the "owner" of the space and the intruder face off, beginning by squirting liquid out of their eyes. This liquid contains information about the lobster for its opponent: size, gender, aggressiveness, as well as several other things. This may be enough to discourage either lobster to back off. If not, the lobsters go into battle, where one of them will come out the loser.

But here's the interesting thing. The brain of the lobster who loses often cannot deal with the loss. So the brain . . . dissolves! The lobster grows another brain, but this one is what I call a "loser's brain." Even if the crustacean has won many battles before, it will never win another, even against smaller lobsters. Its brain won't let it even try.

You and I are not lobsters, but many of us have that loser's brain. The Bible tells us – no, let's make it personal.

**The Bible says God created YOU in His image! He**

loves YOU, unconditionally. YOU are His masterpiece, and YOU can be victorious in Christ.

So what's the problem? Many of us were told throughout our childhood that we couldn't do anything right; that we were losers; that we didn't know what we were doing. Those negative voices, which were unbiblical -- and therefore wrong, by the way -- influenced us to develop a "loser's brain." But it's important to realize that's not what God has planned for YOU.

This book is designed to grow you a new brain, a new "winner's spirit." Because that's what God designed for YOU!

So, let's get started. Whatever your problem, *we want to give you immediate help.* In a moment, we'll explain how the book works. You'll receive some great tools and a lot of encouragement in the days to come. But if you are currently struggling with depression -- or any other difficult emotion -- you need something to help you right now!

Both Dr. Hennigan (Bruce) and I have struggled with depression in the past, but now we have a plan that allows us to conquer it when depression returns. We will probably continue to fight it in the future. Now, however, through Christ and with this plan, we *know* we will win over depression.

If you're depressed, you may feel alone and misunderstood. Perhaps friends or family members have told you to "cheer up," "think positive," or "quit feeling so sorry for yourself." By their comments, you know they do not understand the seriousness of your problem.

**We understand!**

Depression can often leave you feeling guilty about anything and everything. It can cause you to doubt God's love for you. It can even make you wish life would end.

**We understand!**

That's why we are writing this book for you. We not only know what you're going through;

**We've also discovered some powerful tools that can help you conquer depression ...forever!**

One of the greatest helps we have is the wisdom found in God's Word. Take a moment to read the scriptures below. We'll talk about them later in the week, but right now, only think about what they say to you.

*"Humble yourselves, therefore, under God's mighty hand, that he may lift you up in due time.* ***Cast all your anxiety on him because he cares for you"*** *(1st Peter 5:6-7).*

God loves you! And you can give Him your anxieties because He cares! As you progress through this book, you'll discover how to actually experience this love and care in your own life.

Now let's take a look at the make-up of this book.

First of all, it is divided into thirty chapters or "Days." We have used this term for a reason: though you might enjoy doing so, the book is not designed to be read in one or two sittings. Instead, *Hope Again* should be read one "Day" at a time. These bite-size chunks won't take long to absorb, are easy to digest, and should improve your spiritual and emotional health when taken daily.

For the next thirty days, we are going to be a team. In other words,

***You are not alone*** **in fighting against depression.**

Remember what I said about those who fight depression understanding each other? We know, because we've been there, much of what you're going through, the emotional hurricanes that sometimes threaten to sweep you away, and the incredible guilt that comes with all of this. This understanding unifies us with you, and we pledge to help guide you out of the darkness. But Dr. Hennigan (Bruce) and I want your team to extend far beyond this initial month. So we are going to help you put together a strong team that can stay with you for the rest of your life.

Alone, fighting depression is almost impossible. With a talented, caring team, you can actually win the battle. In opening this book and reading this far, *you've already started winning*. Now, let's finish what we've started!

# KNOWLEDGE IS POWER

In the 1800s, a prominent physician, Ignaz Semmelweis, made an astonishing observation. He noted that women on the obstetrics wards whose babies were delivered by midwives never developed a fever. But, women whose babies were delivered by obstetricians on the same wards often developed a fever and died. The only difference between these two groups: the midwives would deliver one baby and then leave, whereas the obstetricians would deliver several babies in a row and would not wash their hands in between.

Semmelweis conducted an experiment with medical students requiring them to simply wash their hands in between deliveries. "Puerperal fever" virtually disappeared in these women. This discovery had the potential to save hundreds, if not thousands of lives. Unfortunately, the noble physicians of the day were offended at the implication that their hands were the source of this fever. In that society, physicians were regarded as "gentlemen." Gentlemen's hands were never unclean! Thus, Semmelweis was ridiculed, ignored, and fired.

What was the cause of this fever? These obstetricians did not *KNOW* about the microbial world of germs. Unwittingly, they had transmitted death from one patient to another through their contaminated hands.

After the development of the microscope, doctors UNDERSTOOD these unseen harbingers of death. Armed with this new knowledge, physicians finally comprehended the underlying problems and the adoption of sterile technique represented a major step forward in modern medicine. Science now regards Semmelweis as the father of the sterile technique.

*Knowledge is power.*

Through *knowledge,* the physicians were able to understand the underlying cause of these horrible deaths. My goal as a physician is to help you UNDERSTAND the disease of depression. I will do this by helping you gain KNOWLEDGE in the coming days concerning your body and mind's relationships to the processes that bring about clinical depression.

> **Through the process of education, you will become empowered with the WEAPON OF KNOWLEDGE to combat depression.**

Part of our effort to help you with depression will involve the use of **LifeFilters.**

In medicine, filters are used to screen out unwanted microbial life forms to purify water. Without the filters, the water might look pure, but it could harbor deadly bacteria.

Our **LifeFilters** serve a similar purpose, helping you to screen out harmful thinking patterns leading to depression. Without the **LifeFilters**, your life might look good on the outside, but it could harbor negative, self-destructive habits.

To get started, go to our website, conqueringdepression.com, to find the **LifeFilters** you will need for the next thirty days. We have also outlined them within the book if you wish to hand write them for a more personal touch. Each day you will use the card that has the **LifeFilter** (concepts that covered in the daily "The Power to Conquer" and "Knowledge is Power") on one side and a Bible verse on the other side. Think of the verse as a *dose of antibiotic helping you to ward off the infection of depression.*

**By grounding yourself in the Word of God, you will begin empowering yourself spiritually to deal with each day.**

**LifeFilters** are a tool. They remind you, gently, of what you have learned that day.

**Remember, learning leads to *knowledge,* and *knowledge* leads to *understanding.***

**Understanding depression empowers you to defeat it.**

God's Word, **LifeFilters**, a Christian physician and a Christian counselor: this is your team for the next thirty days. Together, we're going to help you learn how to live above your depression!

# LIFEFILTER #1

Today, I:

- Can win the battle against depression, because nothing can separate me from my Champion – God.

- Will believe God loves me, regardless of my emotional outlook!

Scripture To Strengthen Me:

*"I am convinced that nothing can ever separate us from God's love, which Christ Jesus our Lord shows us. We can't be separated by death or life, by angels or rulers, by anything in the present or anything in the future, by forces or powers in the world above or in the world below, or by anything else in creation."* Romans 8:38-39 (GW)

# 2

# DAY TWO

# THE POWER TO CONQUER

Welcome to Day Two! But before we get started, I have an important question to ask you. Did you read the LifeFilter from Day One? Did you look at it at least several times during the day?

Why do I ask that question? Because I know how depressed people think. And, if we're not careful, we will torpedo any chance we have for success. Plus it's *hard* to make any effort – like looking at those LifeFilters!

So, let's get this out in the open right now and begin dealing with it. To understand what's going on and why it's so difficult to do anything, come with me and take a look at a rather unique rat cage. This unlikely place holds, as you've undoubtedly figured out, rats. The stuff of nightmares and horror films, these animals might be furry creatures, but they're not exactly cuddly. Studying them, however, can sometimes reveal interesting insights about ourselves. So let's open the door and enter the cage.

See those two rats over in the corner? One of them, you'll notice, seems depressed. He (or she, I'm never sure when it comes to rats) became like this because of a series of events in an experiment. Scientists did it by yoking the two rats together in the cage with a wheel on one wall. They gave control of the wheel only to the rat on the left. Both rodents, however, received an identical electric shock. The shock stopped only when the rat on the left turned the wheel.

Now for the interesting part. Though the shock begins and ends at the same time for both rats, it is only the one on the right who gets depressed! Why? Because he has no control over his life. He cannot stop the shocks.

Consequently, he quits eating, becomes listless, and shows no interest in his surroundings. The rat on the left, on the other hand, cannot stop the shocks from coming, but he's learned that if he turns the wheel, the pain will stop. In other words,

*He has learned that he cannot control when the pain will come in his life, but he can decide how long that pain will continue.*

There's one more lesson to learn before we leave these rats. Scientists have also discovered if they take the depressed rat on the right and move him to the left – in other words, if they finally put the rat in control of when the shocks will stop – he will never learn the lesson. He has already given up, even when there is a solution at hand. [1]

It's time to leave the rats and go back to our own lives.

This paragraph contains a series of questions I want you to answer as honestly as possible. [Bookmark this page. You might want to come back to these questions and review them from time to time.]

- With which rat do you most identify?
- If a solution to your depression is presented to you, will you take it and use it?

- Are you ready to begin controlling how much pain depression gives you, or have you given up?

Don't miss this: Satan, the master of lies, wants you to be like the rat that has given up. You know those negative voices in your head that push your emotions ever farther down? It's Satan. His voice whispers thoughts to you like this: *"You're never going to get over this. You don't deserve a happy life. Nothing's worked before, so this won't, either. Put aside the book and go back to your old life."*

Remember, Satan hates you! He wants only the worst for you. So, don't listen to his whispers. Instead, put your trust in what God says in the scriptures. Believe them, not your present emotional state.

King David, the author of many of the Psalms, probably struggled with depression. Listen to what he says in one of his songs to God:

*"How long must I wrestle with my thoughts, and day after day have sorrow in my heart?" (Psalm 13:2a).*

Can you identify with David? Everything must have looked bleak and hopeless. David's depression was threatening to overwhelm him.

But verse two is not the end of David's story. Listen to what this great man of God says at the end:

*"But I trust in your unfailing love; my heart rejoices in your salvation" (Psalm 132:5).*

One of David's secrets is this: **he never gave up!** He never quit trusting in God, no matter what his emotional state may have been at the moment.

What was good for King David is also good for you and me.

**Don't give up!** Don't, for one more minute, swallow the lie that you can do nothing about your emotional state. With the weapons, we give you, much of the depression and emotional turmoil you're now facing can be lessened, shortened, or eliminated completely. In the section which follows, Bruce will introduce the first weapon which, properly used, can lead to many more practical helps for depression.

So, get ready to pick up these spiritual weapons and get to work making your life better!

# KNOWLEDGE IS POWER

Do you remember the rats Mark introduced? The rat on the left was able to endure the pain of everyday life without becoming depressed because he had discovered how to stop the pain. We want to give you this same powerful weapon – **knowledge**.

**Depression, properly understood, can be controlled and even overcome.**

So let's begin with a medical lesson that will help you discover if you are truly depressed. Armed with *knowledge*, you can escape depression's cage.

A diagnosis of depressive disorder is made if a person experiences at least **five** of the following nine symptoms (and at least one of them must be either the first or second symptom listed here):

- depressed mood most of the day, nearly every day
- loss of interest or pleasure in most or all activities
- change in appetite or weight
- trouble sleeping or sleeping too much

- sluggish thinking and movement, or restlessness and agitation
- low energy
- thoughts of worthlessness or guilt
- poor concentration
- recurrent thoughts about death or suicide.

If you regularly experience more than **five** of these, understand that you are, or maybe, clinically depressed. But don't let this depress you! Now you "know" your enemy. It is no longer a faceless, terrifying opponent. Not only have you put a name to it, but in the coming days you'll learn depression's weaknesses and how to defeat it.

**Remember, knowledge is power!**

## LIFE FILTER #2

Today, I will:

- Remember: I'm not alone; God is with me. He is stronger than my depression!

- Keep my eyes on God, not the circumstances surrounding me.

Scripture To Strengthen Me:

"But I trust in your unfailing love; my heart rejoices in your salvation." Psalm 13:5

# 3

# DAY THREE

# THE POWER TO CONQUER

Have you ever wanted just to give up and die? Have you ever prayed and asked God to take you out of this world so that you could escape your emotional or physical pain?

I have.

I've also counseled many others who felt the same way. As a matter of fact, one of the greatest men in the Bible, a powerful prophet who did many wonderful things for God, got discouraged and was ready to be taken out of this world.

Read his story below:

Elijah was afraid and ran for his life. When he came to Beersheba in Judah, he left his servant there, while he went a day's journey into the wilderness. He came to a broom tree, sat down under it, and prayed that he might die.

*"I have had enough, LORD," he said. "Take my life; I am no better than my ancestors."* ... *And the word of the LORD came to him: "What are you doing here, Elijah?" He replied, "I have been very zealous for the LORD God Almighty. The Israelites have rejected your covenant, torn down your altars, and put your prophets to death with the sword. I am the only one left, and now they are trying to kill me too." (1 Kings 19:3-4, 9b-10)*

God answered every other prayer of Elijah's that are recorded. **But God didn't answer this prayer!**

Why?

Elijah had his eyes on the difficulties of his circumstances. He should have kept his eyes on God.

The prophet let his emotions interpret the seriousness of the situation. Instead, he should have let God intervene and work His will.

In other words, **Elijah's eyes and emotions gave him a false understanding of what he faced.**

The reality of the situation, according to God, was this: Elijah wasn't alone. Though he didn't know it, God had many others in Israel standing for the Lord. But Elijah's emotions had so narrowed his focus that he could no longer see beyond himself.

**God's power was getting ready to enter the picture and take care of His child. But Elijah was looking through the eyes of hopelessness, instead of the eyes of faith.**

Can you identify with Elijah? If so, then perhaps God is trying to teach you the same thing He taught His prophet. Take a few minutes to review the first two LifeFilters from yesterday but let's add two more to drive home the emphasis of this message:

Remember: you're not alone; God is with you.

**Keep your eyes on God, not on the circumstances surrounding you.**

**God's power can change the situation when He thinks it's time.**

**Your Heavenly Father will take care of you – no matter what.**

# KNOWLEDGE IS POWER

I stood in the observation room, and frankly I was disappointed. On the television, NASA Mission Control looked like it was cavernous. Surprisingly, the room was very small. However, its size did not underestimate its absolute importance to every successful space mission. From these control consoles the individual members comprising NASA's "brain" sent messages to spacecraft as far away as Mars. Amazingly, these exact and precise messages could land a Mars rover the size of a grocery cart from millions of miles away.

As a physician, I feel the same kind of amazement regarding that chunk of nerves and blood vessels that sits on our shoulders – the brain.

The brain is the control center of the body. It sits atop the shoulders like Mission Control, gazing down upon the muscles, sinew, and tissue that comprise us. But, important as the brain is, it cannot exist without all the other organs.

The Bible draws an elegant corollary:

*"Just as a body, though one, has many parts, but all its many parts form one body, so it is with Christ." 1Corinthians 12:12.*

The brain communicates with the rest of the body in two ways. First, through the spinal cord, the brain sends millions of nerve cells into every part of the body. The body can then send impulses back along these nerve cells to the brain.

Second, the body can also communicates with the brain through chemicals, or hormones, secreted into the bloodstream. These chemicals have various effects on the organs of the body and can tell the brain how everything is functioning.

**The body is, in reality, an enormous system of checks and balances.** *If something goes wrong with this system, it can give your mind a "wrong" picture of how you are doing emotionally.*

This interplay between the body and mind is important to understand as we examine the physical and psychological aspects of depression. Together, the body and mind determine how you "feel."

In the days to come, you will learn how the physical condition of your body can affect the function of your brain. Also, you will discover how the brain's function can affect the condition of your body. The two are bound together and their balance – or imbalance – determines your emotional state.

The condition of your body is as important as the condition of your mind. So, be prepared, in the near future, to examine your physical condition in detail. By getting in touch with your physical condition, you will gain more knowledge in the battle against depression. You see, depression is a function of the interplay of your emotional life, your mental life, and your spiritual life. We want you to understand this one irrefutable fact: depression is a function of your mind, body, and soul!

**You must address all three aspects of your existence if you are to conquer depression and find hope again!**

## LIFEFILTER #3

Remember:

- God's power can change the situation when He thinks it's time.

- My Heavenly Father will take care of me – no matter what.

Scripture To Strengthen Me:

"My eyes are ever on the Lord, for only he will release my feet from the snare." Psalm 25:15

# 4

# DAY FOUR

## THE POWER TO CONQUER

Today I'm going to introduce you to one of our "crazy" ideas. When looked at properly, it is possible to say that our -- and your -- depression is a "gift" from God.

*"Hey, wait a minute!"* some of you are saying right now. *"Are you crazy? You don't know how much pain my depression has brought me. There's no way it can be a gift from God!"* Yet, this is a theme Bruce, and I will repeatedly be returning to during the course of this book. We want to show you how to look differently at your depression, begin to see it as a strength, and eventually use it as a weapon for good.

Read the following letter from a man who used the first edition of this book to conquer his horrible case of depression – he was close to suicide:

"I will have to admit that the first time I read the part about thanking God for my depression, I laughed cynically thinking, 'How can I thank God for something that is destroying my life?'

> **But God in HIS goodness showed me that in my weakness, I am strong. God is now using my depression to minister to those who are also going**

> through depression. What a concept that I could not have understood prior to reading your book."

You see, this actually works! Now, let's examine how your depression can be a "gift" from God.

You, above all others, are almost forced to find a solution to the problems of life. Others might not question the foundation of their life – until it's too late. You, on the other hand, have an immediate reason for trying to find the way to true peace. Through depression, God has given you the impetus to discover a close relationship with Him.

Perhaps the following story will better explain this concept to you.

Linda was very pleased with her new condominium. Recently built, the units were attracting people eager to have a quality-constructed home. But as the weeks passed, Linda found an irritating, creaking sound when she walked over one particular area of her bedroom floor. She tried to ignore it, but the sound got worse.

Contacting the builder didn't seem as if it would help; he wasn't very concerned. "Every new building has its own particular noises," he told her.

Just to be on the safe side, however, he came out and inspected her apartment. After cutting a hole in the bedroom floor, he examined the support beams to see if everything was in order.

To his surprise, he discovered that the beams which were supposed to join the floor with the supporting wall had been cut too short. Not only were they barely long enough to reach the support beams, nothing had been used to attach them!

It turns out that the creaking noise Linda had been hearing was the sound of the beams slowly slipping toward the edge of their supports. What would have happened had Linda not heard that creaking sound? Her floor would have eventually caved in, possibly killing her. The bothersome noise not only saved her life, but it also saved the lives of other occupants. After discovering the problem with Linda's condominium, the builder decided to check the other units as well. He discovered the same problem in three other units. [2]

When Linda finally realized what was going on, don't you imagine she thanked God for what formerly had been an annoyance?

*Can you do the same thing with your depression?*

You don't have to say that your depression is wonderful. But can you see it as a constant reminder that you need to stay close to God? If you can do this, **you're taking a first step toward using depression, not letting it use you.**

## KNOWLEDGE IS POWER

First, the nurse attaches metal leads across your chest. Next, a mesh shirt is placed over the leads to keep them in place. Then, you step onto a treadmill. You begin to walk, the speed steadily increasing in increments. The incline increases and now you are walking uphill – faster and faster.

Your physician sits calmly at his console, his eyes constantly shifting from you to the heart monitor in front of him. He watches the electrical changes in your heart as it increasingly suffers more and more stress. His endpoint is simple. Pain. If you experience chest pain, it is a signal to your physician that your heart is diseased. But, the doctor can only produce this pain by pushing your heart to a high level of stress. If there is no chest pain, he knows you can achieve a certain heart rate safely and go just beyond without causing damage. Only under such stress can your physician be sure your heart is strong enough for life.

When you are suffering from depression, you walk into the valley of the shadow of death. Your world crumbles around you; the sky grows dark. You are in PAIN! And like the stress test, no one can walk the treadmill for you. Someone, however, is *with* you. God sits at His console, monitoring your heart.

Cardiologists now recognize the importance of aerobic exercise for a healthy heart. It seems like a paradox. Your heart must undergo stress in order to grow stronger.

As much as you may want to avoid depression, recognize that its stress can produce positive growth. Even as you must push your body to its limits to strengthen muscles, your emotional state pushes you to extremes for you to grow stronger psychologically and spiritually. PAIN is the ultimate motivator.

Remember, like the physician watching the heart monitor, ready to turn off the treadmill at the first sign of disaster;

**God has promised He will never give you more than you can handle.**

Just when you think you can't go on, God will give you the strength to take one more step. We like to think that this book is a part of the strength God is giving you, and one way of His saying, "I love *you!*"

## LIFEFILTER #4

Today,

- I will start using my depression as a reminder to stay close to God.

- When I think I can't go on, instead of getting discouraged, I will turn to God, who will give me the strength to take on more step.

Scripture To Strengthen Me:

*"But he said to me, 'My grace is sufficient for you, for my power is made perfect in weakness.' Therefore I will boast all the more gladly about my weaknesses, so that Christ's power may rest on me. That is why, for Christ's sake, I delight in weaknesses, in insults, in hardships, in persecutions, in difficulties. For when I am weak, then I am strong. 2 Corinthians 12:9-10*

# 5

# DAY FIVE

# THE POWER TO CONQUER

Today, let's get right to the point. There is a sticky question many Christians struggle with:

*Is depression a sin?*

This particular question is posed to me by more people than perhaps any other when trying to understand what is going on emotionally with themselves or with someone close to them. The situation isn't helped by well-meaning Christians who don't understand depression saying things like: "You just need to have more faith." Or "There must be sin in your life or you wouldn't feel like this." And even "If you'd pray harder (read the Bible more, have a deeper walk with the Lord, etc.) you wouldn't have this problem." To someone who already feels guilty about everything, this just piles on even more guilt.

But are they right?

**Is depression a sin, or a picture of sin in our life? I answer that with an unequivocal *NO!***

As you will see, depression can, in many instances, have a physical cause. So, also, can alcoholism and several other things spoken against in the Bible. Follow me closely here: *The tendency towards depression, alcoholism, etc. is not a sin; giving in to them, however, is a sin.*

The alcoholic will probably get drunk when he drinks, so the Christian, who is an alcoholic and wants to stay in God's will makes sure he never takes another drink. He will be tempted from time to time, but in Christ, he has the power to say no to the temptation. Likewise, the person who tends toward depression isn't at fault if his or her emotions begin a downward spiral. However, how he/she responds to that downward spiral will determine if there is sin or not.

When I feel depression beginning to clamp its cold hands upon me, I do several things:

*(1) Above anything else, I make sure I'm still reading my Bible and praying.*

Depression often makes you want to do just the opposite, but: **you have the power, in Christ, to do what God wills.**

Say "no" to your emotions and "yes" to communion with God during these times. Let me emphasize that one more time:

**Say "no" to your emotions and "yes" to communion with God during these times.**

*(2) I thank God for loving me and bringing me through the bout of depression.*

This is important. Both of these first two actions go against what I feel. My depression makes me want to stay away from everyone – including God. And it also makes me feel as if no one could really love me – including God. But in reading the Bible, praying to God, and thanking God for His love, I am saying this: **God's Word, not my present emotional outlook, is my authority.**

In thanking God for bringing me through the depression, I am also exercising my faith in God, and in His Word, precisely at the moment, I don't feel like doing it.

*(3) I try to keep from making any major decision.*

I've learned that life looks a great deal bleaker when I'm depressed. Therefore, any decision I make during this time is bound to be colored by a false sense of what's going on in my relationships, my business, and my family.

Taking these steps actually may allow me to have greater faith than many who never experience depression. That's because: **I thank God for taking care of me and loving me** *even when I can't feel it or see it.*

If that's not a biblical definition of faith, then I don't know what is! For example, look at these verses from the Bible.

> *"Now faith is confidence in what we hope for and assurance about what we do not see. This is what the ancients were commended for." (Hebrews 11:1-2)*
>
> *"We live by faith, not by sight." (2 Corinthians 5:7)*

If, when depressed, you can trust God to take care of the situation and bring you through your bout safely, then you're exercising faith. If you can believe He loves you even when you don't feel loved, that's faith.

**In fact, perhaps the person fighting depression who trusts in God has the greatest faith of all!**

So, your depression is not a sin in and of itself. But how you respond to that depression will determine if you sin or not.

Let's try an experiment. Perhaps, when you feel that horrible, negative emotion coming on, you usually say something like: "Oh no, here it comes again. I'm in for a horrible time." Next time, however, say this instead:

*"Heavenly Father, here is an opportunity for me to show great faith and grow in you. May I be faithful to you during this time."*

It might not stop the depression, but it can surely transform what it does to your life! And it can help you remain true to God even in the midst of emotional storms.

## KNOWLEDGE IS POWER

Imagine a world of darkness. In this world, your senses are limited to sound, smell, taste, and touch. For most of your life, you have spent every day crouched against a rough, stone wall, surrounded by the sound of a milling crowd. You feel the warmth of the sun as it shines on your face, but you cannot see it. And then, a shadow falls across you, bringing welcome coolness. A voice from nearby asks the question you have heard so many times: "Who sinned that this man was born blind? Was it his fault or his parents?"

Paraphrased, you hear, "What did this poor, wretched fool do to deserve a life of misery? Where did he go wrong? What did his parents do that he should suffer like this? What sin in his life has brought him to this life of abject hopelessness?"

Perhaps you have had similar thoughts regarding depression. After all, aren't we meant to be happy and well adjusted all the time? If we are unhappy, we MUST have done something wrong. In Jesus' day, all disease was thought to be traced to sin. The Savior of the world knew this was not true – and He was getting ready to prove it.

The young man mentioned above, of course, is the blind

man from the fifth chapter of the gospel of John. The questioners were Jesus' disciples. Jesus Christ, with the divine knowledge of the Great Physician, spoke some of the most encouraging words of the Bible: "Neither this man nor his parents sinned, but this happened so that the work of God might be displayed in his life."

"Dr. Hennigan, I know you've written a book on depression, but it won't help me. I just don't have enough faith, and if I did, I wouldn't be depressed. I keep asking myself what sin have I committed that has brought me depression?" Many people ask this question. Learn a lesson both from the Bible and from science.

**Let's paraphrase Christ's words and direct them towards you: "Neither you nor your family sins have caused this affection, but this has happened so that the power of God might be displayed in your life."**

The disciples were blind to the reality of the boy's *physical* illness. To them, his blindness was a *spiritual* illness. Imagine their surprise when Jesus put mud on the young man's eyes. How strange did that seem to His disciples? When the young man washed away the mud, he saw a whole new world! His physical disease was cured, and the disciples' eyes were opened to the reality that what they had defined as a spiritual malady was, in fact, a disease to be cured.

Transform your thinking today. Depression is a *physical* illness with grave spiritual implications. Fight the disease. Don't give in to the sin!

## LIFEFILTER #5

Today, I will:

- Recognize depression is an illness that can have a physical basis.

- Get rid of the guilt trip and focus on the cure.

- Remember, God's word, not my present emotional outlook, is my authority.

Scripture To Strengthen Me:

"The sun shall not strike you by day, Nor the moon by night. The LORD shall preserve you from all evil; He shall preserve your soul." Psalm 121:6-7 (NKJV)

# 6

# DAY SIX

# THE POWER TO CONQUER

It happened not far from where I live in central Florida. A car lost control, left the road, and flipped over. A passerby saw the accident and stopped to help. As he tried to get to the woman trapped in the vehicle, another car sped by, hit the Good Samaritan and killed him. Why was the man dead? Because he wanted to do something good. But there's another sad part to the story. No matter where you live, you've probably read about or seen a news story very similar.

It's a fact of life, so we might as face up to it. Bad things sometimes happen to us when it's not our fault. We can be as careful as possible, yet still have no control over the bad actions of others that sometimes spill over into our lives. And when it happens, we're tempted to look up to heaven and ask, "Why, Lord?"

A prophet in the Bible could identify with our feelings of bewilderment and hurt. Habakkuk lived about 2,400 years ago, yet his struggles are as fresh as today's news. Listen to what he says to God:

*"Your eyes are too pure to look on evil; you cannot tolerate*

*wrongdoing. Why then do you tolerate the treacherous? Why are you silent while the wicked swallow up those more righteous than themselves?" (Habakkuk 1:13)*

What does the above passage hint at? It says that good and bad things happen to everyone. Regardless of how you try to control your actions, life, with all its complexity, is going to "swarm all over you" from time to time. Even worse, good things will happen to *really* bad people, individuals who laugh at morals and thumb their nose at God.

There they are with their good looks, great personalities, lots of money, and power. Then, when you look in the mirror, you see someone who loves Jesus, yet struggles against depression and the side-effects that come with it. "God, how can this be happening?" you wonder.

"It's not fair," some wail, never getting beyond being an eternal victim.

"I'm never going to trust anyone, even God, again!" say those who have become bitter because of difficult circumstances.

"I give up. It's useless to fight anymore," moan those who have decided to withdraw their energies from trying to live with a positive attitude.

Which one of these excuses are you using right now? Or is it yet still another I've not mentioned? Whichever one or more excuses you employ doesn't really matter: all of them are wrong.

**God hasn't given us the option of giving up, growing bitter or deciding, in our short frame of reference, what is fair or not.**

Now, take a moment to examine your own attitude. Forget

your emotional outlook. If you're depressed at this moment, try to "climb outside yourself" for a minute and look at your life.

Have you given up? Grown bitter? Become a habitual victim?

While I'm at it, let me throw out one more question for consideration: Why do you love God? Why do you serve Him? In other words, are you going to be faithful to God only when everything goes right? Or do you love Him whatever life may bring your way? After all, God saved you from an eternity in Hell by giving His only, beloved Son. He has a place for you in Heaven forever, where you will have a perfect body, perfect emotions, and perfect relationships.

If God never gave you anything else, wouldn't that be more than enough?

The prophet Habakkuk worked through all his questions about God and decided that he would love God, no matter what. He concludes by saying:

> *"Though the fig tree does not bud and there are no grapes on the vines, though the olive crop fails and the fields produce no food, though there are no sheep in the pen and no cattle in the stalls, yet I will rejoice in the LORD, I will be joyful in God my Savior." (Habakkuk 3:17-18)*

Can you say the same thing to your loving Heavenly Father?

**Can you come to the point where you'll trust Him, no matter how bad the present circumstances might be?**

After all, God has a plan that will eventually bless you greatly if you stay faithful to Him.

If you've been having problems trusting in God when things get bad, confess to the Lord that your attitude has been wrong.

Ask Him to forgive you and to begin changing your attitude ... and thank Him, in advance, for answering your prayer.

There! If you've done that, you have taken another important step toward a healthy emotional state, regardless of the depression. Understand that you will probably have to do this more than once; perhaps many times. Your outlook on life becomes a habit, and most habits are not broken suddenly. But don't give up; keep on giving your attitude to Jesus. It will put you on the path that helps you focus on a loving God, not your present circumstances.

## KNOWLEDGE IS POWER

I sat bolt upright in the bed, gasping for breath.

Our family was vacationing at the beach, our escape from a world of stress. But, as I struggled for breath, the nightmarish conviction seized me. Where had God gone? I couldn't FEEL Him! He wasn't there! I looked at my sleeping wife, and I had the utter conviction that all I believed was false. There was no God. I was just biochemistry, and when I died, life would end. I got up immediately and walked to the bedroom where my two children slept. I looked at their innocent features and felt an emptiness so deep it threatened to suck me into some dark, bottomless abyss.

I walked out to the ocean and watched the dark clouds churn across a gibbous moon and felt the cold waves wash against my feet. From the depths of that ocean, a gnawing thought wormed its way into my mind. You came out of that ocean millions of years ago, Bruce. You are nothing more than glorified goo! There is no God! And, the sooner you accept that the sooner you can get on with what little, pitiful life you have left!

Where was God?

Can you FEEL my utter desperation? My complete isolation? I have never felt more alone in my life. Then, like a sudden gale of wind, God's presence came rushing back, filling me with warmth and breath and life. That empty feeling only lasted a few minutes, but it shook me to my core. I had never felt such empty, devastating emotions before. In the aftermath, I descended into a dark depression.

Weeks later, when I finally discussed the incident with my wife, she pointed out an adverse reaction to a medication I had once experienced that left me with similar feelings. Suddenly, I realized I had started taking the same medication just days before our vacation. *The incident was directly related to the chemical changes in my brain caused by the side effects of the medication.* A few years later, that same medication was removed from the marketplace because it caused "sudden and profound bouts of intermittent psychosis."

Depression is considered an illness of the mind. However, it can be caused or accentuated by abnormalities of the body. In fact, certain medications can *cause* depression.

Part of learning how to cope with depression will be a health inventory. Take some time today to stop and look at your health status:

- **Do you have a regular physician?**
- **If so, when was the last time you had a physical examination?**
- **Are you on any medication?**
- **Is there a history of depression in your family?**
- **Do you suffer from a chronic illness or fibromyalgia?**

As soon as you can get an appointment, I want you to commit to undergo a good physical examination by a physician. If you do not have one, choose a physician who has training in family medicine or internal medicine. Once you see him or her, do not be ashamed to share your concerns about your depression. Many types of depression are directly related to a medication or a treatable physical condition. Also, severe forms of depression may require prescription medication (we'll talk more about that in the coming days).

When choosing or re-acquainting yourself with your physician, view your relationship with him/her as a PARTNERSHIP in treating and conquering your depression. Do not be afraid to ask questions and request that this medical professional spend ample time with you. There are many sources of help for depression in the health field.

With the help of your physician, you can learn more about your current health status and better understand the cause of your depression.

## LIFE FILTER #6

Today, I will:

- Love God and trust Him, no matter what life may bring.

- Partner with a physician to determine the status of my health.

Scripture To Strengthen Me:

*"For this reason I suffer as I do. However, I'm not ashamed. I know whom I trust. I'm convinced that he is able to protect what he had entrusted to me until that day." 2 Timothy 1:12 (GW)*

# 7

**DAY SEVEN**

# THE POWER TO CONQUER

Today, we invite you to relax. Relax in the reality of God's love for you.

There is a museum in a castle in Arstetten, Austria which holds a very interesting exhibit aptly titled *Thron oder Liebe.* The translation is "The Throne of Love." The subject of this exhibit is Franz Ferdinand.

Ferdinand was, at one time, heir to the throne of Austria. A problem, however, stood in the way of his happiness. He had fallen in love with Sophie, a young woman who was a "commoner." Permission had been reluctantly given for him to marry her, but there would be a price to pay for his love. He was told that if he did marry Sophie, she would never be empress, their children could never inherit the throne, and they could never claim the name "Hapsburg." Ferdinand married Sophie anyway and lived happily with her until his death.[3]

*Such is the power of love.*

Jesus Christ, God's Son, also gave up a throne. And He did it for *you*. The cross is God's way of saying, "I love *you!*" How great is this love?

**When Jesus learned that the price of loving *you* was to be death on the cross, He said, "I choose the cross."**

*Such is the power of love.*

God's Word puts it this way:

> *"In your relationships with one another, have the same mindset as Christ Jesus: Who, being in very nature God, did not consider equality with God something to be used to his own advantage; rather, he made himself nothing by taking the very nature of a servant, being made in human likeness. And being found in appearance as a man, he humbled himself by becoming obedient to death—even death on a cross! Therefore God exalted him to the highest place and gave him the name that is above every name, that at the name of Jesus every knee should bow, in heaven and on earth and under the earth, and every tongue acknowledge that Jesus Christ is Lord, to the glory of God the Father." Philippians2:5-11)*

Imagine: Jesus Christ, fully God, allowed Himself to become a weak, defenseless baby; He allowed those closest to Him to betray and deny Him at the toughest point in His earthly life; and, most importantly, He went to the cross and died – all alone. Why did He do all this?

*Because He loves you!*

Yes, God loves you, even with your faults and weaknesses!

Have you thanked God recently for loving you? Have you ever simply trusted and relaxed in His love?

Take a moment to put aside the distractions of life. Ignore the worries that sap your energy and time. Focus, instead, on your Heavenly Father. Concentrate on His wondrous love for you. Marvel on the fact that God sees every one of your faults and weaknesses, and yet loves you infinitely more than you will ever understand this side of heaven.

Now, take a deep breath, let it out, and sink down into the marvelous pool of divine love. It is deep enough to hold you, wide enough to encompass you, and pure enough to give you strength, hope, and forgiveness.

***SUCH IS THE POWER OF LOVE – GOD'S LOVE -- FOR <u>YOU</u>!***

# KNOWLEDGE IS POWER

The creation account of Genesis contains a curious description. In Genesis 1:2, the Spirit of God is seen "hovering" over the waters. The original Hebrew word translated as "hovering" is the concept of "brooding," much as a mother hen might brood over her eggs. The Spirit of God brooded over the waters of primitive earth. Imagine His power, His majesty, His glory as He gazed down on the chaos of Earth's early oceans!

Earlier, I shared an incident at the beach that was the beginning of my deep, dark depression. For years after that incident, I refused to vacation near the ocean. Although I loved the beach, the threat of the resurfacing of those painful emotions kept me from returning. Since that time, I have studied the field of "apologetics" or the defense of the Christian faith. I have replaced many of our society's "lies" with the truth of God's creation, God's word, God's unfailing love. You see, our faith in God relies on more than just "blind belief." We establish our faith in the knowledge and evidence that the God of the Bible exists and is intimately involved in our lives.

Now, thanks to God, an understanding of my body, a new way of thinking, and **LifeFilters**, I am better suited than ever to deal with depression. The disease still lurks in the dark corners of my mind, but I have learned that God and I, together, can fight it and win.

When I feel the cold, clammy embrace of depression descending, I recall the Spirit of God brooding over the chaotic waters.

**But chaos did not win the day!**

God's very spoken words would transform this dark, formless watery void into a world teeming with life and light and beauty! On that day, God spoke and in a creation event mirroring His great love and concern for us, brought life into existence in the warm embraces of earth's waters.

A few years ago, I returned to the ocean. On a dark, rain-filled night, I stood on the wet sands and watched the same clouds tumble across the horizon I had seen on that fateful night years ago. I watched the same gibbous moon eclipsed by storm clouds. This time, however, I relaxed, stepping into the same waters once touched by the hands of God. The waters did not mock me. The waters comforted me.

"I made this ocean," God whispered. "I created the moon and the stars," God told me.

"I made the sand on which you stand, and I know each and every grain," God said.

"And I made you. Now, stand here in awe of My power. Look upon My creation and marvel that I did all of this because I LOVE YOU!"

At that moment, I fell to my knees in the surf, awestruck and amazed at God's powerful love for ME! Like His spirit bringing life to this cosmos, His presence brought hope back into my tortured soul.

Today, relax and reach out with your senses to a waiting God who wants to touch the chaotic clouds within your mind and bring new life, new order to your soul.

He is there behind the clouds of your confusion and pain.

He is there beneath the waters that threaten to drown you in despair.

He is there waiting, patient, kind, and loving.

Accept His healing touch today!

## LIFEFILTER #7

Remember to:

- Ignore the worries that sap my energy and time.

- Focus on my Heavenly Father.

- Believe that God loves me, even with my faults and weaknesses.

Scripture To Strengthen Me:

*"Come to me, all you who are weary and burdened, and I will give you rest."* Matthew 11:28

## SECTION TWO

HOW DID I GET HERE?

Not long ago, I was invited to speak at a couples' retreat. The location, a remote camp, had as its address: "the middle of nowhere." At least, that's where it seemed to me to be located! One of the camp employees offered to lead me in his car to the camp, with me following in mine. It took about an hour, with many turns and miles of dirt roads, some without road signs.

When we finally arrived, the director welcomed me and asked, "Do you think you can get back by yourself?"

I looked around at the beautiful – and remote – surroundings. Mentally, I tried to picture our route from the city to the camp. Finally, I shook my head. "I'm not sure where I am," I confessed. "I don't know how I got here. And I definitely don't know how to get back!"

Perhaps that's your situation, as well. Plagued by depression, paralyzed by fears of inadequacy, you are living a life you never expected or wanted. "How did I get here?" you wonder.

For some of you, a difficult childhood put you on this path. For others, an event, or a series of events, opened the gate for depression. And for many readers, a chemical imbalance in your body is playing havoc with your emotions.

That's why, in the coming days, we will explore how you can learn to embrace your past – after all, it's a part of you – and begin using it as a force for God. In other words, triumph, not terror, can be yours, *regardless of your past*.

All of this starts, however, with learning how to build a strong foundation.

What do you do when bad weather hits your area? Many of us watched, horrified, as Katrina destroyed much of New Orleans and the Gulf Coast. Superstorm Sandy bludgeoned the North East, causing millions of dollars of damage and claiming lives.

Several years before those disasters, the infamous Hurricane Andrew slammed into Florida, killing many people, wounding hundreds more, and causing wide-spread destruction. In one south Florida town, television cameras recorded a lone house standing firm on its foundation, surrounded by the debris of neighboring houses flattened in the horrific storm.

"Why is your house the only one still standing?" a reporter asked the home's owner. "How did you escape the severe damage of the hurricane?"

"I built this house myself. And I built it according to the Florida state building code," the man replied. "When the code called for 2x6 roof trusses, I used 2x6 roof trusses. I was told that a house built according to code could withstand a hurricane. I did, and it did. I suppose no one else around here followed the code."[4]

Many lives have been built on lots of different foundations. Some are built on money and the acquisition of things. Others are constructed on personal power. Still, others depend on the accolades of an admiring public.

When the sun is shining, the breezes are gentle, and everything looks rosy, the quality of the foundation you have might not seem important. But when the storms of life hit – when the bitter, cold gales of depression whip against and around you –

your foundation had better be sure. Those who bask in the sunshine might get away with not examining their foundation very often. But for those of us who "walk into the wind" nearly every day, keeping our foundation strong and stable is a matter of utmost urgency.

**In the coming days, Bruce and I are going to help you take the first step in having the wonderful future talked about in God's Word.**

We're going to help you examine your foundation. If it's bad, we'll show you how to replace it. If it has cracks in it because of neglect, in the coming days, we'll teach you how to repair it. And then, together, we'll trust in God to fulfill every one of the promises you've just read.

Now, turn the page and get ready to construct a foundation that can withstand – and conquer – depression.

# 8

## DAY EIGHT

# THE POWER TO CONQUER

In one of my pastorates, I had a member who attended our Saturday night services. Johnny (whose name I have changed to protect him) sat close to the front, and nearly every week, he wore a T-shirt with a different logo or message. One night, in the middle of my sermon, I glanced down and happened to read his shirt. It so startled me I almost stopped preaching. I wanted to laugh but knew that was not the moment to do so.

I grabbed the man after the service and said, "Johnny, from now on, come show me your shirt before the service starts! That way, I won't be distracted by what it says." He agreed, and we had a good laugh. The message on the shirt that almost stopped my sermon was this: "I know the voices aren't real, but they're starting to make sense!"

What voices are you listening to?

Believe me; I've talked to hundreds of depressed individuals over the years. Some are coping well; most are struggling. What makes the difference? How do you move from struggling to being a conqueror? It all depends on what voices you choose to listen to.

You see, we struggle when we listen to the wrong voices.

- Some people listen to the voice of their emotions. They believe whatever emotion is currently in control. When they feel good (which is seldom, if they fight depression), then everything is good. If they feel bad or "down," then no one loves them, God is far away, and nothing is going to work outright.
- Other individuals listen to the voices of the current culture. They allow television shows, social media, or their favorite magazines to determine how they should feel or how they should make moral choices. These people may claim to be believers, but they allow unbelievers to guide how they live! People like this lead lives that are unstable but don't realize why.
- Still, others listen to the voices of their friends and acquaintances. While this is not necessarily bad (we will talk later in the book about how this can be a godly help), those who rely too heavily on these voices find themselves held hostage to ever-changing popular opinion. They have ceded control over their lives to others, always wanting to please someone else. This is a recipe for low self-esteem and little or no peace in life.

So, what voices should we listen to? It's actually one voice – the voice of God. And He speaks to us through His holy scriptures. There are two key differences between the Lord's voice and all the other voices I've described:

- God's voice never changes! He doesn't tell you one thing today and then change His mind the next day. God's voice is consistent, and we can trust it.
- God's voice always speaks **absolute truth**.

The other voices – your emotions, society, even friends and acquaintances – will sometimes be **wrong!**

*In other words, tune out the babble and listen to the Bible.*

It will never lead you astray if you apply its truths to your life, no matter what your present situation might be. Let's look again at several verses we read earlier to see and hear what God is saying to us right now:

> *"Humble yourselves, therefore, under God's mighty hand, that he may lift you up in due time. Cast all your anxiety on him because he cares for you. Be self-controlled and alert. Your enemy the devil prowls around like a roaring lion looking for someone to devour. Resist him, standing firm in the faith, because you know that your brothers throughout the world are undergoing the same kind of sufferings. And the God of all grace, who called you to his eternal glory in Christ, after you have suffered a little while, **will himself restore you and make you strong, firm and steadfast.**"* (1 Peter 5:6–10, NIV84)

God's Word is filled with promises for *you*. And these verses are no exceptions. As you read them, believe that God *will* make them come to pass in your own life. Now, let's recap what these verses say about you and God:

- Being humble is good; God will eventually *lift you up!* (Vs. 6);
- You can give God your anxieties, because He really *cares for you!* (Vs. 7);
- Though Satan is powerful, resting in Christ means *you and God* will defeat him (Vss. 8-9);
- Though you may feel weak and incompetent now,

God *will* eventually make you strong, firm, and steadfast! (Vs. 10).

Now that's what I call a strong message! Wouldn't you like to have this kind of assurance in your life? It comes from deciding which voice will be your source of authority. So, what will it be: your constantly changing emotions, or God's unchanging love for you; society's latest ideas about right and wrong, or God's eternal truths? It's your choice. When you decide to choose God's voice as the One you want controlling your life, you will take a great step toward beginning to control your depression, instead of letting it control you.

**TRUTH ALERT:** mastery over whatever has plagued you for so long won't happen overnight. However, your decision to listen to God above anything or anyone else *puts you immediately on the right path!* This means that eventually, learning to listen to God moment by moment, you *will* win the battle over depression.

# KNOWLEDGE IS POWER

One of my favorite destinations for relaxation and play is south Florida. I can tell you exactly how to get there from my front door. In fact, from my hometown in Northern Louisiana, you can drive nonstop on an interstate highway to Orlando, Florida. Get out the sunscreen and put on your sunglasses. We're going on vacation!

At the first intersection with Interstate 49, take the exit going south. As you increase your speed, notice how quickly the trees and pastures whiz past. Isn't it great being able to stay on the interstate! Before long, you pass beneath an overpass where another intersecting road crosses your pathway. In fact, during the first hour of your journey, you pass under a dozen such intersections, each connecting to a road that leads to a different destination. Fortunately, since you are on the interstate, you do not have to slow down for these intersections. You continue to speed right along beneath each overpass without even blinking an eye.

As you near south Louisiana, you make a turn eastward onto Interstate 10. Up until this moment, the journey has been smooth and uneventful. No difficulties have hampered your progress. Your speed is perfect, and you anticipate arriving in South Florida by nighttime. You dream of awakening the next day, refreshed and rested, ready to hit the beaches.

Your reverie is suddenly interrupted by a detour sign. It seems that at the upcoming intersection, a portion of the highway is missing just beneath the overpass. All traffic is being routed up the off-ramp, through a stoplight, and back down the on-ramp onto the interstate. You slow down, waiting behind other cars. Tension mounts as you wait and wait, motionless. Finally, after what seems an interminable delay, you pass through the stoplight at the top of the overpass and make your way down the on-ramp and back onto the interstate. In moments, you leave the broken intersection behind, already delayed on your journey.

Then things begin to get *worse*.

As the next overpass appears in the distance, you notice a line of cars slowing down. Just as on the previous intersection, the highway is once again damaged beneath the overpass. This time, you wait in line for ten minutes. Ten minutes to traverse one hundred feet because ten feet of the highway is missing!

Soon, you realize your journey eastward contains a damaged segment at every overpass! Your speedy journey has suddenly slowed to a crawl. At this rate, you may finally arrive in Florida, but it will take your entire vacation!

Think of the interstate system I've just described as an interior map of *you*.

A complex, intersecting system of nerve cells connects your mind to your body. At the intersection of the axon -- or nerve "highway" – with other axons, there is an overpass: an intersection where two cells almost touch. The bridge between them, like the ten feet of concrete in the intersection, comes about because of the presence of a chemical called a *neurotransmitter*. This chemical provides the connection between the long stretches of nerve highways.

In depression, these bridges become damaged, just as in the interstate illustration. The bridges are damaged because of a deficiency in a neurotransmitter made, not of concrete, but such chemicals like serotonin. The nerve impulse that drives your body, that is the very core of your thinking, that allows you to feel, is slowed down to such a degree that all the "traffic" grinds to a near halt.

**So you can begin to see how** *the levels of these neurotransmitters are the key to the cause of depression.*

What can cause a change in these levels? What breaks the ten-foot connection at the overpasses?

The causes of depression are numerous. For example, depression can be inherited: in these cases, an inborn genetic problem of abnormal neurotransmitter levels is passed from generation to generation. Depression can also be caused by other chemical imbalances in the body brought on by disease states such as chronic illness or altered hormone function. A classic example is hypothyroidism, a state in which your thyroid gland decides to take a siesta and the rest of the body and mind follow suit.

Several special situations are associated with depression. These are conditions associated with childbirth, advanced age, adolescence, child abuse, drug and alcohol abuse, and gender. Sometimes the underlying cause is related to cultural influences. Causes of depression can be broken down into **nature** or **nurture**. Genetic and medical causes can lead to depression. And, experiences during your life as early as childhood can lay the foundation for depression. Many times, both of these contribute to depression.

As we explore the nature of depression in the coming days, we will touch on some of these special cases. But for now, recognize that just as it takes time to repair the broken roadway before traffic flow can be restored, it takes time to restore the proper balance and level of your neurotransmitters. Sometimes you have to remind yourself of this when you're waiting in line for the traffic to clear.

**Remember,** *be patient as the repair work is being completed!*

As we have said, Knowledge is Power, and we want you to transform your thinking by giving you from this day forward a *Weapon of Knowledge*. That's right! Knowledge will now become your weapon against depression! As you learn more about depression, your *Weapon of Knowledge* is becoming more powerful. And as your base of knowledge expands, you will become more and more proficient at using this marvelous weapon to combat a disease that may have been unfamiliar to you.

# LIFEFILTER #8

Today, I will:

- Listen to God's voice, not my emotions or Satan's lies.

- Thank God that I will be in His hands forever.

Scripture To Strengthen Me:

*"My sheep listen to my voice; I know them, and they follow me. I give them eternal life, and they shall never perish; no one will snatch them out of my hand." John 10:27–28*

# 9

# DAY NINE

# THE POWER TO CONQUER

The enemies you can neither see nor understand have the power to terrify. Nameless fears will awaken you, heart pounding. You don't know what the problem is, but *you know it's coming for you!*

I can still remember those nights when, as a child, I knew something existed under my bed or in my closet. I was sure it would attack me as soon as I closed my eyes. Irrational fears transformed the branches of the crape myrtle tree scraping against my window into a burglar trying to get into the bedroom.

With the passing of years, my bedroom no longer holds those unknown terrors. Now I'm the one trying to comfort the fears of young ones in the bedroom down the hall. But the principle of the unknown still holds true for all of us:

*That which we cannot see and do not understand holds the power to terrorize us.*

That is why Bruce and I are spending so much time on helping you understand how, as a depressed person, you got to this point. Depression can be terrifying to the person overwhelmed by hopelessness, guilt, and despair. **Once the mask of this disease is ripped off, however, it becomes far easier both to deal with and live with.** Again, Bruce and I speak from ongoing personal experience.

Can you identify with the small boy in his bed one night when a violent storm began? As the lightning flashed and the thunder rolled outside his window, the boy began to cry out for someone to help. Just down the hall, the father smiled and shook his head. He knew there was no danger. Trying to calm his son, he said, "Don't worry; you're not alone. You know God is right there in the room with you."

A moment of silence passed, then lightning and thunder shook the sky. The father heard his boy cry out again. This time the boy said, "Daddy, I know God is here with me. But right now, I need someone who has skin on!"[5]

This small child needed someone he could see, feel, and trust, who could take away the terror of the unknown and the nightmares of his imagination.

That's what we are attempting to do for you during these days together. We want you to learn all the symptoms of a depression which may frighten you because you do not understand it. We want to take away the mystery – and the terror – of depression. We want to help you, our teammate, continue to build this wonderful *Weapon of Knowledge*. With it, you will construct a lifestyle and mental attitude that can hold the "beast" at bay.

Before we leave this section, let's return to the story about the boy for a moment. Did you know that Jesus Christ is God with "skin on!" If you desire to know more about the character of God, look at the life of Jesus. He is the One who healed the lepers, cared about the social outcasts, gave a prostitute both forgiveness and dignity, and wept over the sins and hurts of all of us.

Look at what happened to one man who came to Jesus:

*Then a man with a serious skin disease came to Him and, on his knees, begged Him: 'If You are willing, You can make me clean.' Moved with compassion, Jesus reached out His hand and touched him. 'I am willing,' He told him. 'Be made clean.'" (Mark 1:40-41, HCSB)*

Looking for a God with "some skin on?" Then look again at those words, "Moved with compassion." Come and give your fears, guilt, and hopelessness to Jesus. As He looked at the outcast leper, He will look at you. As you ask for help, Christ, moved with compassion, will say, "I am willing. Be clean!"

**Perhaps you have prayed multiple times for help with your depression.** *This book may be God's way of answering your prayers.*

I do know it's His will that you conquer your depression! Don't give up. Don't quit reading. Work all the way through this book and put into place a plan that will help you *the rest of your life.*

## KNOWLEDGE IS POWER

As a child, I marveled at a movie in which a submarine manned by scientists was miniaturized and sent on a "fantastic voyage" into the body of a dying scientist. To understand depression, let's use our imaginations to take a similar journey. Grab your lunch and fasten your seat belts. We're going on a fantastic voyage!

The first thing you notice as we enter the brain area is the clear fluid in which our submersible is traveling. You are looking through what is called "cerebrospinal fluid." This mixture of water, chemicals, and oxygen sustain and maintains the function of the nerve cells. Look to your right. See that tangle of brown ropes? It looks sort of like the chewing gum you stepped on last week, including the little tentacles that stretched from the bottom of your shoe to the street. If you look closely, you will see millions of these bizarre shapes floating in the fluid, each one with dozens of tentacles stretching out in all directions toward each other. What you are looking at are neurons; each of its tentacles is called an "axon."

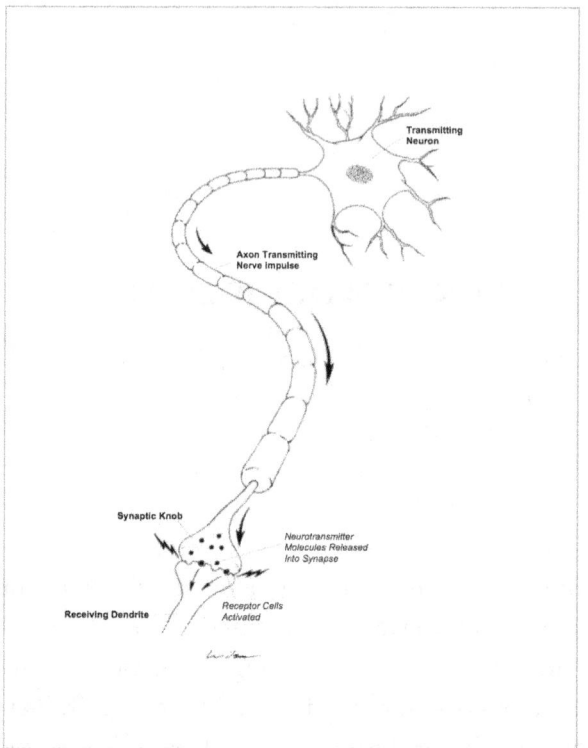

See that sudden flash? It looked like lightning, didn't it? In reality, it was a flicker of electricity coursing down an axon. You've just witnessed the propagation of a nerve impulse. Now watch closely where one axon meets another. Did you see the flicker jump from one axon to another?

Let's move our submersible right next to two adjoining axons. To get a better look at them, let's fire up the molecular magnifier. Screen on! Look at the view now. See how each axon is an appendage containing fluid and chemicals? It's sort of like a pantyhose filled with root beer-colored Jell-O®. (Sorry! I forgot some of you have weak stomachs). Look closely, and you will see tiny pores at the end of the axon.

Now it's time for some "hands-on" experience. Let's take this thin piece of plastic and go outside the ship. Swim over to the spot where there are two axons right in front of you: the end of one and the beginning of another. Now take the paper-thin piece of plastic and slide it between them. Congratulations, you did it! That means there is a gap between the two axons that is so small it is almost nonexistent. This gap is called a synapse.

Now turn on the molecular magnifier in your helmet and take a closer look at the synapse. See those tiny holes in the end of the axon? Watch them closely, because here comes another spark of electricity. Continue to watch as it gets near the end of the axon. There, gushing out of the pores. See the glowing chemicals? Now watch the electric impulse.

Snap!

See how the impulse jumps from one axon to the next through the chemical cloud? You have just witnessed a nerve impulse traveling from some higher function brain cell to another.

Right now we'd better back up a bit, or we'll be swept up in the swirling dots of green coming toward us. Their job is to gobble up the cloud of chemicals. These dots are "enzymes" that clear the chemical, or neurotransmitter, from the synapse. If this weren't done, the axons might become short-circuited, allowing unwanted impulses to race around the brain in total confusion.

Swim this way and examine with me what looks like a "sick" synapse. Here comes a nerve impulse toward it. Watch carefully, and you will notice only a *small* cloud of chemicals issues from the pores. Too bad! That means there is an insufficient quantity of the chemicals to allow the impulse to jump the gap. The electrical impulse can't cross the gap just as in our previous chapter; we saw how your car could not traverse the gap beneath an overpass. Imagine all of these synapses failing to allow an electric current to pass. What you are looking at is a case of depleted neurotransmitter that is causing this brain to suffer from depression.

Let's try to fix it. Wouldn't it be wonderful if we could cure this person of depression right now! Remember how we had problems with the interstate a couple of days ago? Think of us as the Synapse Highway Repair Team. But how can we get these neurotransmitters to do their job? The simplest way is to put up what I'll call "blockades" around the synapse. Okay, team, help me spread them out.

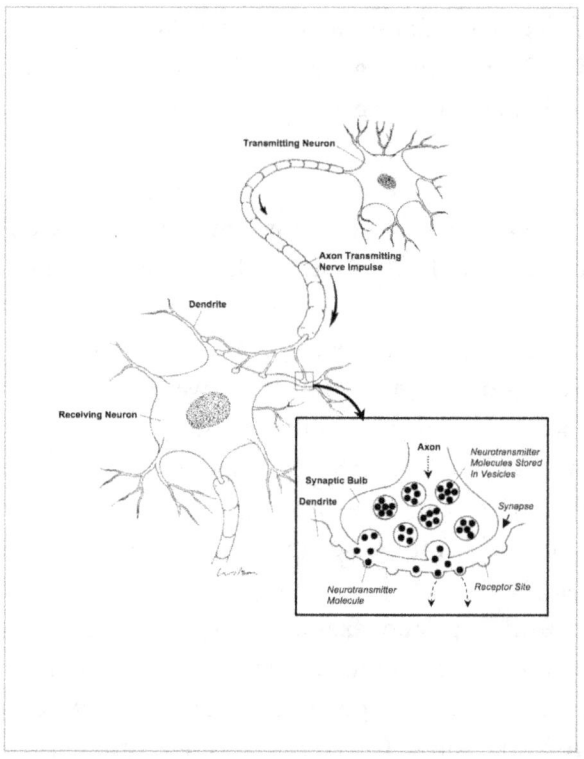

Why are we doing this? So that the neurotransmitter eating enzymes will be blocked off. Watch as the enzymes try to get through the blockade to gobble up the neurotransmitters. But it looks as if we've been successful! The blockade has held them off, and the cloud of neurotransmitter is growing with each attempted nerve impulse. Watch as this time; the electric impulse can make it. The gap has been successfully bridged. The deficient neurotransmitter level has been restored to normal! Congratulations, my friend, for you now can be officially labeled Captain Antidepressant!

I see some of you want to know what makes up these blockades. They've been constructed from antidepressant medication. Now, when the next impulse comes along, there will be extra neurotransmitters left behind to help the nerve impulse make the proper connection.

A quick glance at my air gauge tells me our oxygen is beginning to run low in the survival suits. Let's return to the submersible and review our findings over a mini-sub sandwich (sorry, couldn't resist).

Antidepressant medications work by blocking the enzymes that clear out the neurotransmitters. In this way, necessary chemicals such as serotonin increase their level, repairing the damaged synapse. Why are there so many different antidepressants? Because each medication may act on the same neurotransmitter, but each also has a subtly unique action.

As we pull back, you notice a portion of the brain near its base that has a strange appearance. This portion of the brain is elongated and a bit plump. If you squint and use your imagination, it might resemble a large aquatic mammal.

In recent years, scientists have discovered that in some people, portions of the brain are underdeveloped, and this part of the brain is known as the hippocampus. No, this is not a large mammal rampaging around a college campus! The hippocampus sits on either side at the base of your brain and is involved in learning, memory, and emotion. In some people with depression, we have discovered the hippocampus is smaller than normal. Emotional stress is felt to be a possible cause of this because stress can suppress neurogenesis or the formation of new neurons. Yes, you have a hungry, hungry hippo! And antidepressant medications promote the growth of neurons! It takes time, but these medications take time to form and grow new nerve connections.

This is probably one of the most unique settings you've ever had for eating lunch. It's time now, however, to stop and digest what you've learned.

**Your *Weapon of Knowledge* today is a better understanding of what happens in your brain not only when you are thinking normally, but when depression settles in.**

# LIFEFILTER #9

Today:

- I refuse to let the fear of depression terrorize me anymore. I will, instead, trust in the love of Jesus, who gave His life for me.

- I will remember there are physical and emotional reasons for my depression *that can – and will – be overcome.*

Scripture To Strengthen Me:

*"So do not fear, for I am with you; do not be dismayed, for I am your God. I will strengthen you and help you; I will uphold you with my righteous right hand." Isaiah 41:10*

# 10

**DAY TEN**

# THE POWER TO CONQUER

Matthew Henry's Commentary has blessed and informed thousands of Christians for decades. Many years ago, Henry was held up and robbed. That evening he made the following entry in his diary:

"Let me be thankful—
first, because I was never robbed before
second, because although they took my wallet, they did not take my life
third, because although they took my all, it was not much
and fourth, because it was I who was robbed, not I who robbed."[6]

Is it any wonder Matthew Henry became a spiritual giant who influenced generations of Christians? Early in life, he learned to look for God's exit sign that showed the way out of the rooms of guilt and anger.

If he had wanted, Henry could have engaged in endless speculation after the robbery. *If only I'd been more careful, this wouldn't have happened. God must be punishing me for some sin I'm not aware of. I should never have had this much money on me. I'm *just not supposed to feel safe in this world.* And the list goes on and on until guilt has swept in and covered the whole incident with paranoia and self-recriminations.

Others, whom we'll call perpetual victims, might have said some other things about the incident:

- Doesn't that robber know I needed that money? I'll hate him 'till the day I die.
- I'll relive this incident over and over, and I'll tell my friends about it until they're sick of the subject. After all, my friends should have been with me this evening. I was alone, so it's their fault for not being there.
- Come to think of it, God could have stopped this, but He didn't. It's really all His fault. I'm so angry.

Guilt and anger. For so many people, these are the only responses they know to their own failures and trials. Isn't it interesting that in reading the book of Acts, little of either emotion is found:

- Stephen, a godly man, is stoned to death. As he faces the end of his life, all he reveals is compassion for his accusers and joy at being able to suffer for Christ.
- Peter and John are put in prison for talking about Jesus. They are threatened with death, beaten, and finally released. Did they go straight to their lawyers to sue? Of course not! Instead, they went straight to the temple to praise God for allowing them to suffer for Him.
- James the Apostle is killed. Barnabas is beaten. Paul is stoned, shipwrecked, and imprisoned. None of these even begin to question themselves or God over

the pain they've suffered. Instead, all of them look forward to a future with God. The past, with its mistakes, is given to Christ. The present is lived with full attention to the marvelous, everyday possibilities of God's wonders living in His children.

Look one more time at the two sets of examples above. What a difference! I'm going to ask you three very important questions. Think carefully about each one.

First question: Of the two lists, which attitudes do you want in your life when difficult times occur?

Second question: How do you treat your own failures, mess-ups, and mistakes? Do you agonize endlessly over them? Do you chastise yourself repeatedly and build layer upon layer of guilt in your life?

Third question: How do you deal with things that are done to you, unfairly? Do you become angry and unwilling to forgive? Do you engage in long "pity parties" for days or weeks at a time? Does your family have to tip-toe around you when you're in one of your "moods?"

Depression thrives on guilt and anger. They are the meat and potatoes of this debilitating condition. But don't despair! I'm getting ready to show you several exit signs that lead directly out of the gloomy, joyless rooms of guilt and anger.

Guilt's exit sign is found in Isaiah 43:25,

*"I, even I, am he who blots out your transgressions, for my own sake, and remembers your sins no more."*

In other words, when you bring your sins to Jesus Christ and ask for cleansing and forgiveness, He grants your request. But in addition, He also blots out your sins and remembers them *no more!* Isn't that great! No more guilt or recriminations about how you did wrong at some point in your life. No more tears over lost opportunities. No more losing the "what-if" game over and over.

If God forgets your sins, don't you think it's about time you did, too? Let go of the guilt and embrace a future with God in control and ready to bless you.

Now, what about the anger? Here's what God has to say about this insidious, joy-sapping emotion: "And when you stand praying, if you hold anything against anyone, forgive him, so that your Father in heaven may forgive you your sins" (Mark 11:25).

Do you realize how radical a command Jesus makes here? **Everything** anyone has ever done to you must be forgiven. You can't hold grudges in your heart or bricks in your hand to use against others. A clenched jaw or a clenched fist is not compatible with being in God's will. But the bottom line is this:

*As long as you don't forgive others, you won't receive God's forgiveness!*

Think about that for a moment. You can go to church, contribute heavily, teach a Bible class, even preach glorious sermons from a pulpit. But if you harbor an unforgiving spirit, none of those other deeds means anything! You must forgive others to be forgiven.

Decide right now to begin forgiving everyone. That doesn't mean you allow people to walk all over you; nor does it mean you condone what's been done to you. It does means that you will no longer keep the memory of what these people have done to you close to your chest. Instead, you both free yourself from the chain of hatred and you turn the people who have hurt you over to God's care. Believe me; He can deal with them far better than you can!

Guilt and anger. Some stay locked in these rooms all their

life, never seeing God's exit signs glowing in the emotional darkness.

You have been shown where the exit signs are. Now, what are you going to do with that knowledge?

*Dear Lord...*
  *Please grant that I shall*
  *Never waste my pain; for...*
  *To fail without learning,*
  *To fall without getting up,*
  *To sin without overcoming,*
  *To be hurt without forgiving,*
  *To be discontent without improving,*
  *To be crushed without becoming more caring,*
  *To suffer without growing more sensitive,*
  *Makes of suffering a senseless, futile exercise,*
  *A tragic loss,*
  *And of pain,*
  *The greatest waste of all.*
  Dick Innes[6]

# KNOWLEDGE IS POWER

Let me introduce you to one of my medical school professors: Dr. Molly Cule, imminent professor of biochemistry: the chemistry of life! As she takes the podium, we might get a little nervous at all the information about to come our way.

"Yesterday, you went on a field trip and witnessed the cause of depression," she says. "Hopefully, you now understand the principle of the synapse and the role that neurotransmitters play in keeping the thoughts flowing in your brain. So, today, we are going to talk all about one of those important neurotransmitters."

Dr. Molly Cule is here to introduce Captain Antidepressant and all of his classmates to the almost magical neurotransmitter, serotonin. If you haven't heard about this "neurotransmitter" by now, you will hear more about it as you battle depression. Most of the newer anti-depressant medications work by their effect on serotonin levels in the brain. Serotonin is very important in understanding and overcoming depression.

Let's begin by joining Dr. Molly Cule in the Biochemistry lab and see what we can learn about serotonin. Our professor is holding a model of two nerve endings very close to each other. Remember the "synapse" we talked about on our "fantastic voyage" into the brain? As Dr. Cule introduces a chemical substance into the gap between the nerve endings, we see the spark of a nerve impulse jump from one nerve ending to the next. The chemical facilitating the nerve impulse conduction across the synapse is called a *neurotransmitter*. Now, Dr. Cule pulls down a list of other neurotransmitters that work hand in hand with serotonin such as acetylcholine, dopamine, gamma-aminobutyric acid (GABA), glutamate, and norepinephrine. What a mouthful of words! But don't worry. They all function similarly to facilitate synaptic function.

Dr. Molly Cule is quick to point to a chart listing the benefits of neurotransmitters. They allow us to think, perceive, and move. Serotonin, the neurotransmitter we are most interested in, also controls the regulation of the contraction and expansion of blood vessels; the contraction of the "smooth muscles" of our intestines that aid digestion by pushing food through the gastrointestinal tract; and the function of the "platelets," a component of blood that initiates blood clotting. So, without serotonin, the king of the neurotransmitters, we wouldn't be able to survive very long.

Now, Dr. Molly Cule is pointing to a diagram of the brain and its connections to the spinal cord. See the long set of nerve cells that extends from the brain all the way out to the body? These nerves are called the "serotonin system," and they extend from the brain to the body, composing the single largest system in the brain. This "system" influences a broad range of basic functions from movement to mood.

Aah... Mood is what we are interested in! But did you catch that this system also affects *movement?*

You can now appreciate how a loss of serotonin function can lower the mood and produce depression, as well as lowering the level of movement throughout the body. This results in your feeling "down," and at the same time having a loss of energy, increasing sleepiness, weight gain, and sluggishness. In fact, serotonin is only one of dozens of neurotransmitters that all have differing levels of effect. These numerous neurotransmitters all work together in a system of checks and balances.

Now Dr. Molly Cule is pointing to a group of musicians waiting in the next room. You may want to cover your ears. It seems the musicians are all playing a different song. The sound is horrible! Dr. Molly Cule saves the day by entering the room, rapping her baton on the podium and taking control of the orchestra.

Whew! That's much better. Now all of the musicians are playing the same song, at the same tempo, under the direction of our multi-talented professor. As Thomas Carew, a Yale researcher, commented, "Serotonin is only one of the molecules of the orchestra. But rather than being the trumpet or cello player, it's the bandleader who choreographs the output of the brain."[7]

Let's leave Dr. Molly Cule to her music and continue our exploration of the effects of serotonin. Evidence gained from scientific studies now indicates that low moods -- or depression -- and low serotonin go together. It seems the normal role of serotonin is to balance and adjust our normal mood shifts. It has a role in "habituation," the process in which the brain learns that a particular recurring sensation is not all that important and should be ignored. It's a little like when you've heard a noise in the background, and you've grown used to it. You don't realize it is still there until someone new to your situation points it out. This has happened to me with my children's incessant talking!

When the serotonin system is functioning normally, it helps us keep a steady frame of mind in the face of all of the occurrences around us. It helps us "tune out" the unimportant stuff and respond in a balanced way to the things that matter.

You can see how the balance of the effects of serotonin in your brain and the effects of your environment work together to determine your "mood." Scientific researchers, such as Dr. Molly Cule, who has returned from her orchestra, are discovering much about the chemistry of life and diseases. But do not forget the other half of the equation: your environment, lifestyle, and experiences are just as great an influence. Notice what Dr. Molly Cule is writing on the blackboard.

**Chemistry + Events = Mood + Behavior.**

For instance, scientists now understand that emotional stress sets off a chain of chemical reactions in the body. And, when the stress is chronic, these systems can get stuck in "overdrive."

When a stressful situation occurs, Dr. Cule informs us, another part of the brain known as the hypothalamus (that lives very close to the hippos!) produces a potent hormone known as corticotropin-releasing hormone (CRH). This triggers the adrenal glands and the pituitary gland to release cortisol. Cortisol is like an emergency preparation system and gets you ready to either stand and "fight" or turn and run away in "flight." Your heart beats faster, your breathing quickens, and you become more alert. The downside is that cortisol also affects the brain involved in mood. And here is the crux of the matter, Dr. Cule tells us. With protracted stress, cortisol levels rise too often and stay high, and this leads to high blood pressure, immune suppression, asthma, and possibly depression. All of these effects are related to how cortisol affects the levels of serotonin and other neurotransmitters in the brain.

Dr. Cule reminds us of the interactivity of the entire body with the brain. Once again, we are reminded of the system of checks and balances. The body and brain connection are intricate and affect every thought and every action. Fortunately, Dr. Molly Cule informs us, we will not have a pop quiz!

But, Dr. Molly Cule hopes you can understand the necessity of addressing not only your behavioral patterns, and how they enter into this equation, but also the chemistry of your brain.

**Your *Weapon of Knowledge* today is: *You may need both medication and counseling.***

We will talk more about counseling later in the book, but know the two go hand in hand like the members of an orchestra. Seek to address both sides of the equation, and you may find a new, depression-free balance in your life.

## LIFE FILTER #10

Today:

- Since God has forgiven me of my past, I will let the past go.

- I will ask God to help me forgive others as He has forgiven me.

Scripture To Strengthen Me:

*"I, even I, am he who blots out your transgressions, for my own sake, and remembers your sins no more." Isaiah 43:25*

# 11

# DAY ELEVEN

# THE POWER TO CONQUER

Donna and I married later in life. Both of us lost our first spouses to death, and then we found one another. I was pastoring a rapidly growing church, and so, after the honeymoon, we plunged right into about as hectic a schedule as you could have. She is a cardiac nurse, so both of us were working long hours. We treasured – and still treasure – our free time together.

In any case, we began the process of setting up housekeeping and learning one another's' habits. One day Donna came home from grocery shopping. She started setting out the various items she'd bought, then said, "I got some Jiff Creamy Peanut Butter. Do you like that?" Now, I actually prefer Jiff Crunchy Peanut Butter, but I thought, *she obviously loves creamy, and I'm okay with it, so I won't say anything.*

So I responded with a nod. "Sure, that's fine." Now flash forward seven years. One day, as she left to go shopping, I said, "Buy two jars of peanut butter today: a creamy for you and a jar of crunchy for me."

She looked shocked. "You like Crunchy Peanut Butter?"

"I like both," I said, "but I prefer crunchy."

She started laughing. "I like it too, but I bought creamy because I thought that's what you wanted." Seven years we went like that!!! Both of us just wanted to please the other.

Pleasing the one you love isn't bad. But many people with depression have let this quality run wild in their life. It controls them. They are desperate to please others, even at the expense of doing something they don't want to do. They just can't say no.

Am I talking about you? For example, someone might ask you to do something inappropriate, but you can't find it in your heart to say no, even if you know it may cause you much harm. Because you don't want anyone to be mad at you or disappointed; you swallow hard and say, "Yes, I'll do it." In the process, your self-image plummets, and your depression deepens. The worst thing is: if someone makes another inappropriate request, you'll acquiesce again . . . And again and again.

Inappropriate requests can cover a multitude of situations.

For example you are bone tired and need rest. The person who is asking you to do something either has the time to do it themselves, or there are others they can ask. Will you take their place anyway?

Another example: you have worked hard to get your part of a project done. A lazy coworker who has not done their part now asks you for help at the last instant. Will you rescue them?

The last scenario: an acquaintance who is not good with money asks you for a loan or, worse, a gift. You know they have wasted money, or they have not worked at a job when they could. Will you give in to them anyway?

In other words, in all of the above situations, *will you let others use you?*

Think about your self-image for a moment. Are you so

dependent upon the approval of others that you must ignore what your conscience or body tells you and give in to unreasonable requests? After all, your friends certainly don't have a problem saying "no." You hear them say it all the time – probably to you. So why can't you do the same thing?

If you think it's wrong to say "no," then let me set you straight. God has given you both a brain and the ability to use it. He has promised to place His Spirit in your life to help you know what is right and what is wrong. Maybe you don't want to say, "no" and hurt someone's feelings. But think about this for a moment:

*When you say, "yes," to inappropriate requests, you are actually saying, "no," to God's Spirit within you and denying the quality of the intelligence He gave you!*

Jesus never let the expectations of others determine His actions. Take, for example, an incident at the beginning of His earthly ministry. He had begun speaking and healing in the region of Galilee. Because of their willingness to believe, the people saw mighty miracles when they brought the blind, lame, and deaf to Jesus. The message quickly spread throughout the area that a wonderful miracle worker was in their midst. It culminated in the following incident:

*"That evening after sunset, the people brought to Jesus all the sick and demon-possessed. The whole town gathered at the door, and Jesus healed many who had various diseases." (Mark 1:32-34)*

Now, the next day has dawned. Excitement among the people has risen to a fever pitch as they make their way toward the house where Jesus is staying. The crowds swell. Perhaps merchants set up their booths in anticipation of a busy day with a hungry crowd. Adrenaline flows strong in the veins of the disciples. They talk excitedly among themselves about the future of Jesus and their place in that future. As the popularity of their Master grows, they will be a part of it!

The noise of the crowd around the house where Jesus and His followers have spent the night is now so loud that conversation is impossible. The knocks begin; the people are excited; the needs are urgent.

If you were Christ, what would you do?

The verses following those we've just read give us a brief but startling response by the Son of God:

> *"Very early in the morning, while it was still dark, Jesus got up, left the house and went off to a solitary place, where he prayed. Simon and his companions went to look for him, and when they found him, they exclaimed: 'Everyone is looking for you!'*
>
> *"Jesus replied, 'Let us go somewhere else—to the nearby villages—so I can preach there also. That is why I have come.'" (Mark 1:35-38)*

What was Jesus thinking? There were people at the house waiting to be healed. Steadily gathering crowds were eagerly anticipating a glimpse of Him so they could give Him adulation. The world, at least in Galilee, was His for the taking.

**But Jesus didn't let others' agendas determine what He knew was wrong and right.**

Let's take a moment to examine why Jesus acted as He did:

- He knew the importance of spiritual refreshment. Regular, uninterrupted time with God was so

important to Him that it superseded everything else.
- He knew that filling others' needs was no substitute for doing God's Will in His own life.
- Jesus refused to let anyone's definition of "urgent" take the place of what He knew was right for Himself. (Please read that sentence again!)

We can learn some important principles for our own life in looking at Christ's life.

If anyone ever loved others, it was Jesus. He had not only created everyone with whom He came in contact. He also knew one day He would die for them! But that did not keep Him from saying, "no" to their requests from time to time. In fact, sometimes saying, "no" can be one of the most loving things you do! True love does not repeatedly rescue someone from the consequences of their bad behavior. This only enables the person to continue their sinful lifestyle and make you feel used. True love forgives, but it also encourages positive change by allowing the person to discover why they need to change and move toward God and His will.

Remember this incident from the life of Jesus the next time someone asks you to do something you believe would not be good. If you say, "no," several things will happen.

- First, to your astonishment, the world will not stop.
- Second, the person asking will still be your friend (if they break off the relationship because of this, there was no "friend" relationship to begin with; it was only a "user" relationship for them).
- Third, your self-esteem will begin going up as you are true to what you believe to be right – and better self-esteem means a happier person.
- And don't miss the bottom line in all this: a rise in

self-esteem makes you better able to fight off the effects of depression.

What Jesus did can also be a part of your own life. Take the Weapon of "No!" and use it to fight off inappropriate requests. You'll discover that using this powerful weapon has made you stronger and depression weaker.

## KNOWLEDGE IS POWER

For many years I ran two to six miles a day. As I aged and my back began to protest, my running devolved into fast walking. On a cool, late spring day, I was into the last fifteen minutes of my one-hour walks. The sky was bright blue. Flowers bloomed all around me as I walked through my neighborhood. It was a beautiful day until a fist began to close around my heart.

I paused and leaned against a tree and began gasping for breath. Was I having a heart attack? After all, I am a doctor, and I should know. I had not brought my cell phone with me. Sweat began to pour down my chest. Nearby, a man working in his yard approached. He asked if I needed help, and I borrowed his cell phone to call my wife.

In fifteen minutes, I was lying on a stretcher in the emergency room with a dozen people swarming around me like ants in a disturbed ant pile. IVs. Oxygen. Nitro paste. Blood drawing. If my chest tightness wasn't enough, these ministrations might do me in! Later, my doctor asked if I wanted to undergo a treadmill test or a cardiac catheterization. I wanted to know for sure. Get out the catheters!

My cardiologist took only eleven minutes to perform the catheterization and leaned over me in the cath lab with wonderful news. "Bruce, your coronary arteries are big enough to drive a truck through. You're fine."

Now, I'm a worrier. I was born that way! So, if my coronary arteries were normal, then where had the chest tightness and chest pain come from? The answer came from my wife. She is the wisest person on the face of the planet. I, on the other hand, not so. Why? Because I keep forgetting to listen to her!

In the months before my heart episode, several things had happened in my life. Two of my partners had retired, and we had increased our workload at the hospital by much more than fifty percent! And, we had to take more after-hours and weekend call. And, I had agreed to help out with a drama worship service for children at church. And, I had signed a five-book deal and was finishing my second manuscript, prepping the rough draft for the third, and planning the fourth book. And, I had to build a website and social media for the books. And my wife and I had to make some decisions regarding caring for our daughter with epilepsy. And, my mother in law had moved in with us, and she suffered from dementia. And, my father, a robust 97-year-old, was romancing up to five women at church and his nursing home. And, well you get the picture.

My wife patted me on the hand. "Your heart is fine. It's just your lifestyle that isn't. You've got to learn to say, NO."

I was exhausted!

**The warning signs were all around me, and I did not see them. Instead, I was listening to other voices pleading for my attention.**

I realized that I had fallen into the trap of saying "yes" to any voice that called out my name. Here's the humbling part of this realization. This very same behavior was the chief contributing factor to my first descent into depression. After two years of counseling, I thought I had learned my lesson! What did I learn?

I had come to the realization that I could not say "no." Always saying "yes" to what seemed like good ideas had led me to overextend myself physically, mentally, emotionally, and technologically. Notice that last word. Technology.

Let's face it. As intense as requests for our time may be from the people around us, nothing compares to the magnification of the frequency and urgency of those requests thanks to the tyranny of "screens" in our life. Dozens of these technological voices scream for our attention.

Smartphones. Tablets. Laptops. Cable television. Netflix. Hulu. Facebook. Twitter. Pinterest. Tumblr. Texting. Snapchat. YouTube. Just to name a few. Screen after screen after screen flickers and pulses its clarion call for our undivided attention!

Information is all around us, overflowing, gushing, flooding our minds with the clarion call to KNOW! Know it now! Know it completely! Don't get left, "uninformed." Information is merely a click away, and it produces a not so subtle pressure to always be in the know. A neurosurgeon recently told me there is an epidemic of herniated discs in the neck because people are now constantly looking down at their cell phones. They can't say "no" to a simple text! Let's face it; it is almost impossible to be unplugged in our society!

Alvin Toffler, in his 1970 book, *Future Shock* predicted "information overload," and today it is epidemic. Our brains can only process so much information, and a recent study showed that we are exposed to almost 50 GB of new data every day.

And, herein lies the problem. When the brain is trying to process too much information, stress occurs. Mental stress triggers the "flight or fight" response. Remember, Dr. Molly Cule referred to this response? What is this phenomenon?

Imagine you are walking down a dark alleyway. Okay, so anyone in their right mind would never willy-nilly walk down a dark alleyway, but suppose for some reason you do. From behind a dumpster stumbles a disjointed, bleeding zombie. He shuffles toward you, groaning and reaching out so he can snack on your flesh.

Instantly, your brain realizes you are in imminent danger. Adrenaline surges and prepares the body to "stand and fight" or to "turn tail and run." In either case, large quantities of adrenaline flood the body. And, the body cannot sustain prolonged adrenaline surges. This phenomenon accounted for the chest pain and anxiety I had experienced that fateful night. I wanted to run, but there was nowhere to run! I wanted to fight, but there was no one to fight!

Let's look at the *fight* response. How does this lead to depression? You can't get into a fight every time your brain is overloaded. But, your brain thinks it is time to fight. Being the humane, civilized person you are, you hold it in, and the overload turns to anxiety. Prolonged anxiety, as we shall see, leads to depression.

What about the *flight* response? You can't physically run away from your mind. But you can run away from the world deeper *into* your mind. You can withdraw into yourself! You focus inward all of the details of this problem and soon, you develop feelings of hopelessness and inadequacy.

Lucy Jo Palladion, Ph. D. says, "When overload is chronic, you live in a state of unresolved stress and anxiety that you can't meet ongoing demands to process information."[8]

What is one to do in a world inundated with data? What is one to do when voices cry out for you to say "yes" to every request?

**First**, recognize that information overload is epidemic in our society. It is an unavoidable situation. It is the nature of our existence. The voices are there! This is particularly true of our young people and young adults. They were born in an age when they have spent all of their time "online." Those of us who are "digital adopters" grew up "offline." As we will discuss in later chapters, we must help those who have never been "offline," such as our teenagers, to learn how to create real relationships. Those of us who learned how to get "online" must help those of the digital age learn how to live "offline"!

**Second,** realize that the brain can only process so much information without undergoing potentially disastrous changes in brain chemistry. This is why sleep is so essential to your continue sanity (We will talk more about sleep later!). Technology is killing us! The need to keep abreast of **everything** is destroying our minds and souls.

**Third,** information overload can produce *analysis paralysis*. You are unable to weigh all the possible outcomes, and often, you choose the worst possible solution. This is how fast-food restaurants manage to stay in business. This is why you say "Yes!" when you should be saying "No!"

For now, I want you to stop and think about all of the data streams in your life. If you are depressed, then there is a tendency to pull away from any form of interaction. But, I am talking about those noisy, raucous sources of information clamoring for your attention. It could very well be that paying attention to all of these technological "voices" in your life has contributed to your depression. Recent studies have shown that even though we are more connected than ever, we are the loneliest individuals in the history of America.

Take a deep breath and do something very simple. Take a walk. Get away from the smartphone, the tablet, the laptop, the television for just a few minutes and see what happens. Allow your brain to relax, to lower its oven setting to "simmer" instead of "broil." Learn to use the word "no" to the incessant voices.

In the coming days, we will explore some concrete steps you can take to overcome the influence of information overload in your life. For now, it will be enough to be aware of this phenomenon. Learn to say "No" to the seemingly good voices in life and say "Yes" to God's voice!

Paul had this advice centuries before his words were incorporated into your Bible app:

> *"We destroy arguments and every lofty opinion raised against the knowledge of God and take every thought captive to obey Christ," 2 Corinthians 10:5 (ESV).*

It is time to take your thoughts captive, to rescue them from the maelstrom of modern-day information overload. Your *Weapon of Knowledge* today leads you to a very important action: unplug from the world and plug into God's word!

**Say NO to the good ideas so you can say YES to the God ideas!**

## LIFEFILTER #11

Today:

- I will not let the agendas of others determine what I know to be right or wrong (i.e., it's okay to say "No!).

- I will unplug from the world and plug into God's word.

Scripture To Strengthen Me:

*"We destroy arguments and every lofty opinion raised against the knowledge of God, and take every thought captive to obey Christ." 2 Corinthians 10:5 (ESV)*

# 12

# DAY TWELVE

# THE POWER TO CONQUER

I hate to tell you this, but it's time to get to work. Yes, I know depression keeps us from wanting to do anything. Maybe just reading this book is about all you think you can do. Nevertheless, I really need you to complete this assignment *today*. It's very important. So, let's start with a question:

What habits do you need to break?

I want you to make a list – actually write down these bad habits. However, before you begin making a list, consider this. Chances are there are some strong habits of which you are completely unaware. And they might be the very ones holding you back from a healthy emotional lifestyle! So let's take an inventory. Get out a piece of paper, grab your pencil, and get ready to think and write.

Wait just a minute -- I know what you may be thinking: *This is hard. I know he said to do it today, but I'll do it another time; maybe tomorrow.* You can't put this off until another time and continue to get better. Don't make excuses; make a list!

Here are some thoughts to get you started.

- **Are there any relationships I am maintaining that**

push me toward negative thinking and depression?

Does God want you to give up these relationships? Are there people you know who cause you to begin thinking in the wrong way? Or, if it's a relative (not a spouse), can you put a little space between you and them from time to time?

- **Are there some activities I engage in which tend to make me depressed? Can I give them up?**

My friends still laugh at me about the way I gave up golf. I'm a pretty hyper person, and at one point in my life, I found myself making excuses about why I couldn't go play eighteen holes with my friends. After analyzing my reaction, I finally saw that the four or five hours I spent playing golf was a huge block of time I didn't want to give up. Also, the game didn't move fast enough to keep me from thinking about things at the office. The result was that I came home from the course tenser than when I started!

One beautiful spring day, I was playing on a championship course with three good friends. I had just hit a four-iron to the edge of the seventh green, and my partner revved up the cart to move us in that direction.

"Larry, pick up my ball, please," I said.

Larry was startled. "Why? What's going on?"

"I'm quitting golf," I replied.

"When?" Larry was becoming more and more puzzled by my behavior.

I grinned and said, "Right now. And I don't think I'll play it ever again until I retire." With that, I got out of the cart, walked to the car, and drove away with a lighter heart than I'd had in a long time. With one exception (for a church tournament), I've not played in years.

Do I think golf is wrong? Of course not! In fact, I still watch it on television and follow it in the sports pages. But golf was wrong for me and my mental health at that point in my life.

It may be an innocent activity, but if something you're doing causes you to be stressed or depressed, and you can quit it, then do so.

- **Have I paid attention to the things that enter my mind through my eyes and ears?**

1) Television: Are the television programs you watch helping you toward a healthy mental outlook? If you watch reality shows, for example, understand that the subject matter is overwhelmingly negative. Secure marriages are seldom presented. Truth and positive lifestyles are in short supply. A steady diet of programs like this can soon make you believe they represent a normal life. The "trash" talk shows are even worse. Hype, not help, is the subject of these programs. I'm convinced every day you spend watching one of these shows moves you closer to depression. Can you change your daily viewing schedule? Or even better, can you eliminate it altogether and replace the viewing time with something more positive and less passive on your part?

2) Movies: Are you indiscriminate in what you watch when it comes to movies? Whether at the theater or at home on cable, there are a host of movies available that cover dark subject matter and present a terrible morality. Watching these shows cannot make you a happier person or a better Christian. Can you be more selective in what you watch?

3) Books: What I read stays with me for a long time. I can remember scenes from favorite books I read twenty years ago. In short, books are powerful. If you read the wrong type, however, you allow an insidious enemy entry into your mind. Once there, it can affect you long after the book is finished and

the pages have been closed. On the other hand, good, encouraging books can also stay with you a long time, working throughout your mind, heart, and emotions to make you a stronger person. Can you choose better books to read and put down the "trash?"

4) Music: Do you ever find yourself humming a tune without realizing it? Music is also a powerful medium. Because the tune can be catchy or beautifully melodic, the message attached to it may stick firmly in your mind. Is the music you listen to moving you closer to God, or farther away from Him? Should you change your listening habits?

- **What are my "Time Wasters?"**

Admittedly, we're beginning to get into the subtle areas of your life now. Time Wasters, however, can not only slow you down, but they can also contribute to your stress level and depression. When you realize you're not going to be on time, or you no longer have the time to do an important task, guilt and disgust are waiting in the wings of your mind to take over control of the emotions

I monitor my behavior carefully when I'm depressed. I've discovered that if I'm not careful, my whole life will crawl to a halt while I engage in navel-gazing or who-knows-what for long periods of time.

The above questions and suggestions should be enough to get you started making a good list of habits which, taken away from your daily life, will actually enrich you. Start writing down your bad habits and Time Wasters!

How did you do? Are there other habits you need to add to the bottom of your list?

The exercise you're currently completing is quite significant. That's because identifying the problems is at least half the battle. You can't fight an enemy you don't know or can't see.

Once it's put down on paper, however, you begin robbing the bad habit of its power.

In Psalm 119:37, we have these words of wisdom:

*"Turn my eyes away from worthless things; preserve my life according to your word."*

Let your eyes – and your ears, mouth, feet, and hands – turn away from worthless, time-wasting, guilt-inducing habits.

As you begin cleansing your life of these distractions, you are better able to see one of the exit signs blinking in your life, offering another way to leave the power of depression behind forever.

Take a moment to ask God's help with any habits that need to be eliminated from your life. You might want to pray:

*Dear God, here are the bad habits I've identified. If there are any others I need to be aware of, please show them to me now. As best I can, I give these habits to You. Please take them away from me and replace them with good, healthy habits. Thank You for hearing this prayer and starting me on the right path. And thank You for loving me in spite of my weaknesses. In Jesus' name, Amen.*

# KNOWLEDGE IS POWER

In 2015 I turned sixty. That fall, I was in the worst physical shape of my life. My father had passed away. My contract for those five books had fallen apart after two books when my publisher decided to dissolve the imprint for those types of stories. Our medical practice had formed a board of directors, and I had assumed the role of Chief Medical Officer. The constant interaction with the hospital administration occupied most of my free time. In times of mental and physical stress, I turn to my one source of comfort. Food! Brownies. Chips. German chocolate cake. Pralines and cream ice cream. Cheesecake. Did I mention brownies?

Ulysses had to resist the call of the sirens, their voices urging him into their hungry arms. My "sirens" were imprisoned safely out of sight. But I knew exactly where they were. They called to me, their promise of fulfillment so powerful an image in my mind that I abandoned all logical thinking. I drifted from the bedroom to the kitchen. I was getting nearer! I could almost feel them in my hands, taste them on my lips.

The brownies cried out for their freedom from bondage!

My wife had made them, and for days, I had avoided them.

After a week, the brownies were dry and stale, and my wife threw them into the trash compactor. Their broken bodies were trapped beneath the flattened lettuce and discarded potato peels, reposing at the bottom of the trash in their package. I pulled out the trash compactor and reasoned only a day's worth of trash lay between me and the brownies. Yes, I dug them out of the trash! And yes, I ate them! Voila! I washed them down with milk!

The call came on a late Wednesday afternoon from my doctor. My lab work from the Monday before showed I was diabetic. My blood sugar was almost 200! Understand that I work on patients in the end stages of diabetes all the time. I interpret their angiograms that show peripheral arterial disease leading to amputation. I interpret their kidney ultrasounds that show the onset of renal failure. I install dialysis catheters for their upcoming dialysis. I know what the end result of diabetes can be. I was more frightened than at any other time in my life. I sat on our couch and cried; no, sobbed for over an hour. What was I to do? My great love was food. My comfort was food. My escape was food! Now, my enemy was food!

For my entire life, submission to this temptation of food was an ongoing sin. In my attempts to avoid overeating, I had been on every diet known to man and then some. I had tried it all, and food was the only thing that soothed me.

**In my moments of deepest, dark despair, food would always be my friend. It filled up my emptiness.**

When I went into my deep depression, my sister made a simple statement. She told me I was depressed because of all of my bad habits and, "Anyone can break a habit in 30 days." That made me pause and consider just what "bad habits" had led me into depression. And, could I break those habits in 30 days? Now, my life depended on breaking those habits!

In his book, *The Power of Habit*, Charles Duhigg shares how researchers at MIT discovered a simple neurological loop at the core of every habit. This "loop" has three components: a cue, a routine, and a reward. This habit loop lies at the heart of a particular behavior. And, that behavior, like binge eating, can be the instigator of depression![9]

In the case of the brownies, my habit loop went like this. Whenever I felt stressed out, I would wander around the house and end up in the kitchen. Stress was my **cue**. Wandering into the kitchen was my **routine**. And there, laid out like the pot of gold at the end of the rainbow, were the brownies, my **reward**. I would eat a brownie and feel full. Not necessarily physically full, but at least the empty, aching feeling of stress and depression was assuaged. This habit began packing on the pounds!

Could I now identify one of these bad habits that had led me to depression? Earlier I mentioned my inability to say "no." That problem lay at the heart of my greatest weakness, low self-esteem. I wanted people to like me. No, I wanted people to *love* me. In my flawed reasoning, if someone needed me, they would have to like me. And if I was available to help someone by saying "yes" to their requests that meant they needed me. Besides, if I said "no," then they wouldn't like me anymore. In fact, they might reject me! And, rejection is the cruelest blow to my ego. And, so, not only did I say "yes" to any and all requests, particularly in my service at church, I went looking for opportunities to promote myself, so I would be asked to serve.

By the time I descended into my deep, dark depression, I was so overextended, so overloaded, so exhausted I no longer had the energy to serve anyone. So, what did I do?

- First, I had to identify the bad habit. I did not know how to say "no." My bad habit was always saying, "yes."
- Second, what was the **cue** that sent me into my habit

loop? The cue was my basic insecurity. I wanted to be loved, to be accepted, to be needed.
- Third, I had to identify the **routine** that allowed my cue to lead to bad behavior. The routine was finding my friends at church.
- Fourth, I had to identify the **reward**. In this case, it was the smile and the acceptance I received when I said "yes." This stoked my ego and assuaged my low self-esteem.

How did I break this bad habit once I went into my depression? I realized I needed a break from the routine that led to this behavior. My wife kicked into protection mode and made sure that I attended only the worship service for the next 30 days. I avoided the hallways and the offices where I might meet someone who would ask me to do something. I altered my **routine**.

The next step was identifying the **cue**. My counselor very wisely told me to ask a simple question whenever I felt inferior. "What is the lie?" This one phrase set me free. It meant that the idea "you are worthless" was a lie! (We'll talk more about lies and truth later.) And, who is the father of lies? That's right! Satan! Talk about time-wasters? Satan had me so wrapped up in his lies that I was exercising these bad habits and wasting God's time for my life! Satan had diverted me from the true path, and I was wandering around in his wilderness of wasted time.

The final step was instituting a substitute for the **reward**. You see, eventually I would be going back to normal activities at my church, and I would be around those people for whom I wanted to say "yes." This was unavoidable. I would be confronted with the same requests that got me where I was in the first place. How was I going to avoid seeking the reward of acceptance?

This is where I developed the idea of **LifeFilters**. My original **LifeFilter** was a card with five questions on it. To offset the reward of unconditional acceptance when I would say "yes," I would pull out the **LifeFilter**. I would pause, read through each question, and tell the person, "If you want an answer right now, it is no. But, if you let me pray about this and talk to my wife and family, I might say yes. Give me 48 hours, and I will let you know the answer."

Habit loop broken! I cannot tell you the joy of watching the stunned expression on the faces of those who would ask me to help out when I did not say "yes." In fact, it was my refusal to give an unconditional "yes" that led Mark Sutton to come to me and demand to see my card. Once he saw the **LifeFilter** and saw the change wrought by breaking this one habit, he asked me to help write a book on depression. And, the rest, as they say, is history! Please know that in learning how to say "no" to all of those good ideas, I was able to say "yes" to God's ideas!

- In summary,
- identify the **routine**,
- experiment with alternate **rewards**,
- isolate the **cue**,
- and develop a **plan** to interrupt the habit loop.

One way you can do this right now is to utilize the **LifeFilters** accompanying this book. Use them to help you interrupt the cycle of your bad habit loop! Use them every day! They are essential in your conquering of depression and finding hope again.

Today's *Weapon of Knowledge* is: Make using your LifeFilter a GOOD daily habit.

When you feel the **cue** of low self-worth, develop the

**routine** of consulting your **LifeFilter** for that day, and the **reward** will be to defeat Satan's lies! And the **truth** will set you free!

After my diagnosis of diabetes, I downloaded an app on my cell phone to track everything I ate. I went to a dietician, and we formulated a diet. Within a month, I had lost twenty pounds, and my glucose was back to normal! In fact, on my return visit at three months after my diagnosis, my doctor said, "Bruce, if I had not seen your lab work three months ago, I would now say you are no longer diabetic. Keep up the good work."

We can overcome the potentially deadly effects of bad habits. Begin the process of breaking the old bad habits and replacing them with new, helpful habits!

## LIFEFILTER #12

Today:

- I will watch out for Time Wasters and try to eliminate them from my daily habits.

- I will ask God to help me "discern what is best" in how I use my time.

Scripture To Strengthen Me:

*"And this is my prayer: that your love may abound more and more in knowledge and depth of insight so that **you may be able to discern what is best** and may be pure and blameless for the day of Christ." Philippians 1:9–10 (emphasis added)*

# 13

## DAY THIRTEEN

# POWER TO CONQUER

"Pastor, I have a gun in my hand. I'm going to put it in my mouth when I hang up the phone, and then I'll pull the trigger." 'Jack' had his share of problems. His mom had committed suicide. His dad had just died. Now, his wife was leaving him.

I scrambled for the right words to say, even as I silently prayed for wisdom. "Jack, don't do this, with the help of God, we can . . . "

"Sorry pastor," Jack interrupted. "It's over. Thanks for all the help."

"Wait!" I shouted. "I'm asking God for a miracle that will stop you, and I'm driving over right now."

The phone clicked dead. As I rushed to my car, I begged God for an immediate miracle. At the end of this section, I'll finish the story.

I've already talked to you about the importance of identifying the voices clamoring for our attention. But today, I want to single out one of those voices. It's the worst of all the other voices. When we hear it initially, it horrifies us. But some who fight depression don't tune out the voice. They keep listening as it whispers in their ears. And the longer they listen, the more logical the voice sounds. If something doesn't change, one day they will give in and obey its seductive beckoning.

It is the voice of suicide.

Make no mistake, for someone who is really in pain, suicide can look like the best way of handling everything. But, what does the voice of suicide whisper? Here are some of its offerings:

- It will take away your pain.
- You won't be a burden on anyone anymore.
- People will be better off without you.
- It is a way out. And you've been looking for an escape.

But, is any of what we've just read true? Is the voice of suicide right? Let's examine that voice, not with our emotions or our present circumstances, but with the ultimate authority, God's word.

*"I can do all things through Christ who strengthens me." (Philippians 4:13, NKJV)*

*"For God gave us a spirit not of fear but of power and love and self-control." (2 Timothy 1:7, ESV)*

*"You shall not murder." (Exodus 20:13, ESV)*

*"I pray that the perception of your mind may be enlightened so you may know what is the hope of His calling, what are the glorious riches of His inheritance among the saints, and what is the immeasurable greatness of His power to us who believe, according to the working of His **vast strength**. He demonstrated this power in the Messiah by raising Him from the dead and seating Him at*

*His right hand in the heavens." (Ephesians 1:18-20, HCSB, emphasis added)*

What do we learn from these passages?

**Above all, we learn that God's power is in every believer, ready to fight our battles for us.**

How strong is that power? It's the same power that raised Jesus from the dead and set Him at God's right hand! In other words, *you*, with God working in you, can overcome all things. Also, you are commanded not to murder, and this includes yourself. You are precious to God, and He has a plan for your life.

If the voice of suicide says just the opposite of these biblical truths, then who is speaking? Make no mistake:

**Satan is the voice of suicide. Satan places those thoughts in your mind. His goal is to hurt you, not help.**

Mark this place in your book. Return to it anytime you begin to have suicidal thoughts.

"But what good am I to anybody?" you may ask. Did you know that simply by resisting suicide, you may be giving strength to someone else who is struggling? **Your willingness to endure and be faithful to God may save someone else's life.**

How do you stay away from suicide?

- I believe it starts with an initial decision: *I will never listen to suicidal thoughts.* God will honor that firm decision and give you His strength.
- Second, retrain your spiritual ears to listen to the voice of God. You do this by reading each day's **LifeFilter** regularly. *This is vital!* Read your

- **LifeFilter** fifteen or twenty times a day. As you do this, you learn to lean on eternal truths, not on present circumstances.
- Above all, since God does not want you to give in to the voice of suicide, you can be sure that when you pray for strength, He *will* hear you.

Now, let's return to Jack. When I reached his house, I could see him sitting with another man on the front steps. They were talking quietly and calmly. As I got closer, I could tell it was Frank, a godly man in our church. "I didn't know you two knew one another," I said.

Frank smiled. "I've never met Jack. I was just driving along and saw him sitting on the porch. Suddenly, I got this overwhelming impression I was to go and talk with him. So I did."

Jack grinned in embarrassment. "Frank's been hearing my story and sharing some helpful scriptures." He shook his head. "I don't know what you prayed, but the miracle sure worked."

Before we leave this section, let's go back and read Ephesians 1:18-20 one more time. Notice these words:

*"His incomparably great power;" "mighty strength." These are available for each of us – for you.*

Remember, God loves you. His voice never changes. Think about this: Jesus may have wanted this chapter written just for *you*! It is Christ's message of hope, strength, and love that He means for you to follow.

# KNOWLEDGE IS POWER

My daughter was eight years old when she had her first seizure. It was my fortieth birthday, and within months, I would spiral downward into depression. The story of my daughter's battle with epilepsy is heartbreaking. She is one of the bravest people I have ever known. She endured ten days of 24 hour EEG monitoring at the age of 9 and again at the age of 26. She suffered through years of medication trials. She faced the social stigma of being different at school. She worked very hard at passing her final exams to graduate from high school. The day she walked across the stage to receive her high school diploma was the greatest day of her life!

But, controlling her seizures had always been difficult. Why? Because the initial diagnosis of the cause of her seizures was wrong. When my daughter entered her twenties, her symptoms changed. After the second round of EEG testing, we discovered that her seizures had changed and, thanks to newer imaging technology, we now have found the source of her seizures. Because of this new knowledge, we changed her medication. Soon, her new symptoms resolved, and now she is moving on with her life. It has been amazing to watch her blossom and to witness her begin to think clearly and to engage the world in her life.

You see now why it is so important to have the correct diagnosis. We have already asked you to take a test to determine if you are depressed. Before we go much farther, we need to talk about the different types of depression. There are different types? Yes, there are, and even this chapter's discussion may reflect a classification that will soon change. However, we will look at the main forms of depression, so you will better understand the type of depression you may be suffering.

**Major Depressive Disorder**

Major depressive disorder has been redefined in the latest psychological manual (DSM-5) as someone suffering the symptoms listed in the test you took on day two. These symptoms are present nearly all day, on most days, and for at least two weeks. Symptoms can also include anxiety, worrying, or distress. Other signs can include a loss of sexual desire, pessimism, hopelessness. Physical symptoms such as headaches, unexplained aches, and pains, or digestive problems.

Episodes of depression frequently recur as about half of those suffering from major depression will have at least one more episode later in life. This type of depression is the most commonly recurring form of this condition. In fact, major depression can be profound and disabling, often preventing the person from functioning as he once did.

**Persistent Depressive Disorder**

Once known as dysthymia, this persistent disorder is the presence of low-level depression that lasts for at least two years. This form of depression lasts an average of five years.

**With this disorder, one feels depressed during most of**

the day, and the depressed mood may not lift for more than two months at a time.

This syndrome begins in childhood, teenage years, or early adulthood.

The changes in persistent depressive disorder are similar to major depression, including changes in appetite, sleep issues, low energy, poor self-esteem, and feeling hopeless. However, the person is able to function more normally, often feeling "down" much of the time.

**Bipolar Disorder**

When depression alternates between intense highs and lows, it is known as bipolar. The low episodes are essentially a major depressive episode. The highs in bipolar disorder are called manic episodes.

**Seasonal Affective Disorder (SAD)**

This form of depression is probably the best known, although you may never have given it a name. It is the "holiday" blues. And, it has a physiologic cause. When changes in the seasons occur, the altered light levels and changing climate conditions can bring about shifts in mood for some people. Most commonly, the symptoms start in the fall and continuing through the winter months. How do changing light levels cause this kind of depression? With the decrease in sunlight, there is a disruption in the levels of melatonin and serotonin in the body.

There is a wide range of the presentation of depression. It ranges from the deeply troubling major depressive disorder to profound manic episodes. The truth is that, like my daughter's seizures, your type of depression may not fit neatly into one of these categories. That is not a real problem. The treatment options are very similar except for manic/depressive disorder.

Your *Weapon of Knowledge* today is slightly different from other days. For, you cannot discover the nature of your depression alone. What is of paramount importance is to understand that the diagnosis and treatment of your depression cannot proceed without professional medical input. As I mentioned in previous days, you must have a team to help you defeat depression.

**Depression is an emotional, physical, and spiritual disease. A doctor is absolutely essential in the diagnosis and treatment process.**

Depression treatment options are so varied and unique; you MUST have the proper diagnosis. Only a qualified health care professional can accomplish this. If you have not done so, now is the time to make an appointment to see your doctor – preferably a "primary" care physician such as an internist, OB/GYN, or family doctor.

**This is not a suggestion. This is an absolutely essential requirement for you to get better.**

Only by partnering with a health care professional can that person give you a clear diagnosis of the type of depression you are suffering from. This is the only way to find your *Weapon of Knowledge. You cannot defeat the enemy until you understand the nature of your depression!*

So here we are close to the end of the second week of your journey in finding hope again. We have seen how neurotransmitters allow the brain to function normally and how defective synapses contribute to the physical, emotional, and spiritual condition of depression. We have seen how habits and information overload in combination with these faulty synapses contribute to depression. We have learned how antidepressant medications restore the chemical balance to your brain. Now, you have seen the wide range of diagnoses in depression. Somewhere in this continuum of depression, you will find yourself. With the *Weapon of Knowledge*, you must move on in finding treatment. Don't waste time treating the wrong kind of depression. Get help today! This can help you begin to conquer depression forever!

## LIFEFILTER #13

Today, I will:

- Refuse to listen to suicidal thoughts. Instead, I will rest in God's love (Psalm 34:18).

- Lean on God's eternal truths, not present circumstances.

Scripture To Strengthen Me:

"The LORD is close to the brokenhearted and saves those who are crushed in spirit." Psalm 34:18 (NIV)

# 14

# DAY FOURTEEN

# THE POWER TO CONQUER

The couple and their young son were getting ready to order their evening meal at a local restaurant. As the parents asked for substitutions and gave careful instructions for the kitchen on their food preparation, the veteran waitress took it all in stride. She had seen it all and was unflappable.

She also had her own ideas about what was right and wrong.

When it was the boy's turn to order, he rushed his words as fast as he could, knowing it was probably futile. "I want a hot dog...."

Before he could say anything else, his parents interrupted, "No hot dog!" The mother began making a substitute order for her son. "Instead, bring him the beef, some vegetables and...."

She stopped in mid-sentence, her mouth open. It was obvious the waitress wasn't even listening to the parents. Calmly, without hurry, she looked at the boy and asked, "What would you like on your hot dog?"

He smiled at her shyly and said, "Just ketchup – and lots of it! And please, could I have some milk?"

"No problem," the waitress said as she turned toward the kitchen, leaving behind her stunned parents and an incredulous boy.

When she had gone, the boy turned to his parents with a big smile and said, "I like her, 'cause she thinks I'm real! She thinks I'm real!"[10]

Do you ever feel like that little boy? You have real longings, unspoken hopes, deep heartaches. Yet when you dare to try to express any of these emotions, perhaps you find others not really listening. Or if they listen, perhaps they are uncomfortable with the subject matter. Instead of taking you seriously and trying to deal with what you've said, they may even try to sweep your moods under a rug, telling you just to forget about them.

You've looked for help. Instead, you've found misunderstanding.

If you can identify at all with what I've just written, then you feel just like many people I counsel. Because they can't take a pill and feel better in thirty minutes, or get an antibiotic shot and be well in four days, most of society doesn't know how to deal with those struggling with depression. So, what happens with many people that follow this scenario:

- There is an initial rush of compassion for the depressed individual from family or friends.
- Much advice is given with confidence – often from people who have never suffered from depression in their life.
- When the advice doesn't work (often because it's wrong advice!), or when the depressed individual doesn't "rejoin" society immediately, those who were formerly caring begin to lose patience. They go on with their lives, leaving you to struggle with yours.

They no longer treat you as a "real" individual.

The widows and orphans of Old Testament times must have felt the same way. These two groups were disenfranchised and endangered. They lived in a harsh time where slavery and cruel deaths were common. There was no Social Security to look after these people, no government programs to ease their burden, no media to bring to light their needs. And so these, the weakest of the weak, suffered horribly, often going to an early death.

Few were willing to treat the widows and orphans as "real" individuals.

It is in this context that God, with the following words, explodes into the midst of an uncaring society and changes the fortunes of the "forgotten ones."

> "A father to the fatherless, a defender of widows, is God in his holy dwelling. God makes a home for the lonely; He leads forth the prisoners with singing." (Psalm 68:5-6a)

When no one cares for society's outcasts, God astounds us by saying, "I care." Our Heavenly Father is a loving, caring parent to all those who never had a good family life. He gives a home in His house with a warm atmosphere to anyone who is lonely. And, finally, God promises to lead you out of your emotional prison and give you joy.

In other words, God cares – for *you*!

**When no one else pays attention to your problems, know that God is right beside you, caring for *you*!**

When it seems as if not another individual can understand the depths of your pain, God is there with perfect understanding, and He cares for *you*!

You and I are like the little boy in the restaurant. We can say,

"I love God. He pays attention to me and cares about my needs. *He thinks I'm real!*"

# KNOWLEDGE IS POWER

Sharon was a delicate child with porcelain skin and pale blue eyes. She would perch on the side of her hospital bed and sing to the robins nesting on the ledge outside her window. Her skin was pale because she had a low blood level. Her blood level was low because her bone marrow was ravaged by leukemia. She was dying.

The reflected sunlight of a beautiful sunset painted her cheeks in a rosy glow that was denied to her by the disease that consumed her body. And yet, she was so full of life; so full of possibilities. My heart was broken, not so much because she was dying, but because her form of leukemia was curable. We had it in our grasp to save this young girl's life, and something was standing in our way.

You've heard this type of story dozens of time: a reliance on faith to heal and a refusal to consider any other form of salvation. How could I reach her parents? How could I break through this barrier to modern medicine? More importantly, how could I, as a Christ-follower, tell these people that sometimes just faith wasn't enough?

The secret lay in my past. As a senior in high school, my

ambition was to become an astronaut. To journey among the stars, seeking out new life and new ... well, you know the rest! I would have happily settled for the job of a chemist, or an astrophysicist, or any scientific position as long as it was *not* in medicine. The last thing I would ever want to be was a doctor.

In the winter of my senior year, my pastor preached the only sermon of his I can still remember. He related how God calls *all* of us to work for Him. Not everyone is a preacher or a missionary. Some of us are called to be good Christian school teachers, godly accountants, or gas station attendants for Christ. The important point is to find where God wants you to be. I was so convicted, I bowed my head and surrendered my future to God.

God spoke to me that day. Not in a thunderous voice from heaven. Not with doves descending or angels singing. In my heart, I knew beyond the shadow of a doubt I was meant to be a doctor. I also found an instant, life-sustaining peace with that decision. As I left the church that cold Sunday morning, I knew where my future lay. There would be obstacles, hard times, and difficulties. But I did not despair. God had decided I was to be an instrument of His healing power.

As I remembered my experience, I sat on the bed next to Sharon and asked her parents to listen to my story. I told them, "You have prayed for God to heal Sharon. If I am called by God as an instrument of His healing, then I may be the answer to your prayer. Will you let God help your daughter through me?"

After praying about it and talking with Sharon, the parents allowed us to proceed with treatment. Somewhere today, years later, I like to think Sharon is showing her daughter the beautiful robins nesting outside her bedroom window.

Shortly before Super Bowl XXXIII Dan Reeves, the coach of the Atlanta Falcons underwent bypass surgery for coronary artery disease. Publicly, he credited Jesus Christ with his recovery. He said God had sent him "angels in white coats" to heal him. As you prepare to be the victor over your depression, please realize God can use doctors and nurses and counselors as His instrument of healing.

Your *Weapon of Knowledge* today is:

**Don't try to do it only on your own. Listen to the wisdom of the Holy Spirit and seek out that health care professional God may have raised up just to take care of you.**

## LIFEFILTER #14

Today, I will remember:

- No matter what I face, God cares for me!

- God also cares for me through the concern and wisdom of other Christians.

- *I am not alone!*

Scripture To Strengthen Me:

*"Cast all your anxiety on him because he cares for you." 1 Peter 5:7*

# SECTION THREE
## WHERE DO I START?

It's time to answer the above question. We're 14 days into our plan for conquering depression and finding hope again. We've learned – and will learn more in the coming days – about depression and how to fight it. But how do we begin moving forward? This might sound contradictory, but we start our journey forward by looking back – in other words, by taking a review.

There was once a farmer who had a very successful dairy business. One day his neighbor came to see him. "Would you mind loaning me some rope for a few days?" he asked.

The dairy farmer was busy with his cows. But he stopped what he was doing and answered, "I have some rope, but I'm afraid I can't loan it to you. I have to use the rope to tie up my milk."

Startled, the neighbor said, "You know that doesn't make any sense!"

The dairy farmer nodded in agreement and explained, "I know it doesn't. *But when you don't want to do something, one excuse is as good as another!*"

"When you don't want to do something, one excuse is as good as another."

With those words in mind, be honest as you answer these questions:

1. Are you reading a chapter in this book every day? Why or why not?
2. Have you begun praying to God every day? Why or why not?
3. Are you beginning to believe that God really loves you, as He promises in the Bible? Why or why not?
4. Are you using your **LifeFilters** every day as a positive reminder? Why or why not?

Please understand, I am not pressing you on these questions in order to add to any load of guilt you already carry. Nor do I want you to feel even more depressed because you can't answer 'yes' to all of the questions! But remember: Bruce and I both know what it is like to be depressed. And we know that state of emotions can paralyze your decision-making ability if you're not careful.

It's easy to make excuses as to why you've not taken the steps recommended already in this book. But be honest; could your reason for not doing it be the same as the dairy farmers? If so, consider this another starting point and ask God to give you the strength to begin taking the above steps to overcome depression.

Again, we know ourselves during depression. We have a tendency to stay frozen in one spot, physically and emotionally.

**But we must continue to remember that *doing nothing different produces nothing different.***

That's where the importance of reviewing becomes so

important. It is so easy to get caught up in each day's emotions and activities. If we're not careful, we can find ourselves swept up and moved far from the goals we had originally set. When we take the time to review, however, we force ourselves to take a long look at the progress we've made – or not made – over the previous days or weeks. It helps us gain perspective and make mid-voyage course corrections before we go too far astray.

Now that you've read the previous paragraph, take another look at the above list of questions. Use them to put your life back on track and to evaluate your progress. And if you see that progress, no matter how small, truly has been made, then thank God for the help and give yourself a congratulatory pat on the back. You deserve it!

But, what happens if you have to admit you've not been doing some or all of the exercises? Three things:

1. Learn from your mistakes and commit to working these steps daily;
2. Pause right now, take your **LifeFilters**, and go over them;
3. When you've finished looking at the **LifeFilters**, ask God to give you His strength to make progress.

Don't dwell on the fact that you haven't done what is necessary. Instead, learn from your mistake and decide to move forward.

Let's close with a reminder from God to all of us about how much He loves even the weakest of us. In this passage, God is the Shepherd; we are the sheep. Perhaps you feel like a baby lamb who is so weak he or she cannot walk one step farther. When you look at other people, often they seem to be strong and incredibly gifted compared to the weaknesses you see in yourself. You might also wonder how God could love you when He has so many able servants.

What does God have to say to someone like you in these circumstances?

*"He tends his flock like a shepherd. He gathers the lambs in his arms and **carries them close to his heart**." (Isaiah 40:11, emphasis added)*

If you feel so feeble that you cannot walk another step in life,

**Rest in the assurance that *God is carrying you* close to His heart right now.**

He has a special love for those who are weak and hurting, but who still love God in spite of their difficulties.

You might want to bow your head at this moment and thank God for His mighty love for *you*.

# 15

Day Fifteen

# THE POWER TO CONQUER

What is the purpose of a powerful weapon? Essentially, it is designed to help you overcome an enemy, win a battle, or provide you with protection. If this is true, then "Meditation" certainly qualifies as one of the most effective weapons in your entire arsenal.

As I begin to discuss this subject with you, however, let me give you a strong word of caution. "Meditation" by itself, can be dangerous. The current trend running through America is that every philosophy, every religion, every person's choice of behavior has equal value. Therefore, the philosophy continues, anything you decide to meditate on will help your sense of inner peace. Bruce and I are convinced that this may be popular, but it is *heresy of the rankest form*. As my Dad used to say to me when I was growing up, "Son, no matter how popular sin is, it's still sin!"

Why do I say it is heresy to believe every philosophy or religion is equally valuable?

First of all, it makes a mockery of the fact that there are non-changeable rights and wrongs, no matter what one particular society or culture may say to the contrary. It also ridicules the necessity of Jesus Christ dying on the cross for our sins. After all, if every religion, every philosophy, and every person's behavior is equally valid, sin can't really be that much of a problem. All one has to do is "be sincere," and everything is okay. In such a "tolerant" milieu, the Son of God's death would really be superfluous. And speaking of sincerity, this line of reasoning is so popular with many people that it elevates "simply being sincere" to an unhealthy level. Sincerity won't stop a bullet, keep the rain off your head, defy the law of gravity or bring you back to life.

Several years ago, a young man from England made headlines around the world because of his misplaced sincerity. He and his girlfriend went to Egypt to visit the ancient pyramids and the Sphinx. There, surrounded by what he believed were "spiritually powerful" artifacts, he jumped from a high building, sure he would be raised from the dead after falling. He wasn't, of course. He learned, too late, that sincerely believing in something that is false will hurt you every time.[11]

Having said all of this, let me now explain what I mean by "meditation." For you, as a Christian who has chosen God's Word as the ultimate source of authority, meditation has three parts:

1. It is time spent thinking about what God has said to you in His Word.
2. It is personalizing the promises of God in the Bible.
3. It is listening for God to speak to you and to strengthen you.

When you begin employing the *Weapon of Meditation*, you also begin winning the battle against the tyranny of your emotions. Left to yourself, your emotions when depressed will give you a false impression of life, your circumstances, your relationships with others, and God's love for you.

**It is only as you allow God's Word to become the authority for every area of your life** –*especially when you are depressed* – **that you begin to correct what is a dark, negative view of life.**

When you meditate on the truths and promises of the Bible, you begin concentrating on the world *outside* your depression. When you meditate on the scriptures, you allow God's medicine of divine love to flow into your depressed emotions, sending healing and peace.

We will examine further the *Weapon of Meditation* tomorrow. I'll give you some tips on how to make the best of your time spent in God's Word, and I'll show you why it's important to have a regular system of Bible reading. For now, however, let's close by meditating on these words from God:

*"The LORD your God is with you; he is mighty to save. He will take great delight in you; he will quiet you with his love; he will rejoice over you with singing." (Zephaniah 3:17)*

Each time it is used, replace the word "you" with the pronoun "me." Then take a moment to thank God for His mighty love of *you*.

# KNOWLEDGE IS POWER

Between my junior and senior year of medical school, I worked in the pulmonary medicine clinic. These specialists treated various types of lung diseases such as emphysema, lung cancer, and asthma. On a hot August afternoon, I examined a young woman having difficulty in adjusting her asthma medication levels. It seemed the medicine she was taking had to be taken in such large doses that she became toxic to the point of vomiting up the dose -- often before it could take effect. She was frustrated because all she wanted was to be able to breathe.

Throwing the weight of my idealistic young mind into the problem, I came up with the perfect solution. I discovered her medication was available as a suppository. Aha! Keeping her medicine down would no longer be a problem. Beaming proudly with youthful ardor, I handed her the new prescription and asked that she return the next week.

A week later, I entered the examination room, expecting to see a transformed woman. Instead, to my horror, her asthma was so out of control; she could barely breathe. I was shocked and dismayed as I listened to her wheezing.

"Did you take the suppositories as I directed?" I asked.

"Yes, doctor." She replied. "I put one up each nostril just like I was supposed to."

I hope you realize suppositories are not administered through the nasal route. But, to this woman, whose problem was her *breathing*, putting the medication up her nose made perfectly good sense.

**I failed to communicate properly with my patient.**

Let me be honest. The doctor-patient relationship isn't as personal as it once was. New regulations and requirements have opened a chasm between you and your doctor. Finding time to create and maintain a close, professional relationship is almost impossible for your physician. Physicians are now answerable to onerous government regulations and paperwork at the expense of time spent with their patients. This is why there are now more "physician extenders," such as physician assistants (P.A.) and nurse practitioners than ever before. More than ever, you must be more proactive and involved in your medical care. You are your own best advocate! Don't be timid or shy. Be bold and assertive. It is your body and mind we are talking about! The days of "I'll do whatever you tell me, doctor, because I trust you," are gone.

Effective medical treatment only works when there is a true partnership between the doctor and patient. It is as important for a physician to clearly communicate your treatment as it is for you to know which questions to ask. As you enter into the healing process of your depression, I want to help you choose a physician and learn how to avoid the pitfalls of poor communication particularly in today's world of fast-paced, highly regulated medicine.

At the forefront of medical care is the primary care physician who may be a family practice doctor, an internist, a pediatrician, or an obstetrician/gynecologist. Primary care physicians are trained in the basics of recognizing, diagnosing, and treating depression. Remember, however, that this is a two-way street. You should be prepared to ask questions regarding your depression.

**Remember, there are NO "stupid" questions. Every question is a valid one if you don't know the answer.**

The most important questions to ask your doctor are:

- Do I have an underlying physical illness that is causing my depression?
- Do I have a chronic medical condition that may be causing my depression?
- Do I need medical treatment, counseling, or both?
- How safe is the medication you would be giving me?
- What are the side effects?
- How long will it take for me to see improvement?
- Are there other alternatives if this medication proves unsuccessful or has undesirable side effects?
- Will this medication interact with other medications I am taking?
- How will medication affect other medical conditions I have?
- How soon will I feel better?
- Are there genetic tests to determine if my depression is inherited?

Once you and your doctor have addressed these physical aspects of your disease, it will be time to determine if you need more specialized treatment under some type of professional counselor. We'll venture into that territory soon. For now, remember the importance of two-way communication.

How do you avoid the trap of the suppository up the nostril?

**Today's *Weapon of Knowledge* is: In choosing a primary care physician, it is of paramount importance to feel you can develop a relationship with this physician.**

**If you cannot, then find another one.** *Never be afraid to change physicians or to insist on all of your questions being answered.*

As a doctor, I can tell you most physicians today welcome an involved, pro-active patient who insists on investing time in their own treatment. Don't be afraid to be strong. In doing this, you are continuing to take charge of depression, instead of letting it take charge of you.

## LIFEFILTER #15

Today, I will:

- Thank God for providing doctors and medicines which can help me.

- Establish and maintain a daily quiet time.

- Stop and thank God for loving me.

Scripture To Strengthen Me:

"The LORD your God is with you, the Mighty Warrior who saves. He will take great delight in you; in his love he will no longer rebuke you, but will rejoice over you with singing." Zephaniah 3:17

# 16

# DAY SIXTEEN

# THE POWER TO CONQUER

Yesterday we introduced the *Weapon of Meditation*. Today we'll learn how to refine and use it properly. We have already established the fact that it is essential for us to read and meditate upon God's Word, the Bible.

One of the questions many people ask me is, "How should I read and study the Bible?" It is best to have some system you stay with on a regular basis. For example, Donna and I read a bible passage and a devotional every morning at breakfast. For us, "Our Daily Bread" is great, but there are also other devotionals you can find.

We also have different ways of having our personal devotions. Donna reads through the Bible in a year. My plan involves separating the Bible into four parts, then reading some from each part daily.

- The first section is from Genesis to Job
- The second section is from Ecclesiastes to Malachi;
- The third section is Matthew to Acts
- The fourth section is Romans to Revelation
- I read just a few verses from Proverbs every day.

- Some days, just one verse. The point is to meditate on it.
- I read Psalms whenever I'm feeling down or need to pour out my heart to God.

I don't try to read a chapter from each section. My goal is to focus on the verses I'm reading and try to apply their truths to my heart.

Another way of Bible reading and meditation is to choose several books of the Bible and read a chapter from each daily. Psalms and the gospel of John would be two good places to start. Proverbs gives you some wonderful promises, and First and Second Peter provide divine counseling for living in difficult times.

Some additional suggestions for applying these scriptures and letting them make a difference in your life:

1) Read the Bible daily – even (and especially) if you don't feel like it.

2) After you've read a chapter, ask yourself several questions:

- "What has God taught me in this chapter?
- What promise has God given me in these verses?
- How can what I've learned affect my life today?"

3) If a verse you've read is especially meaningful to you, write it down and try to memorize it, carrying it with you for several days.

4) Take a moment to pray after each session:

- thank God for His constant love;

- pray for someone in need;
- ask God to take care of your needs;
- tell Him of any specific problems you are facing, and trust Him to take care of them in His own time and in His way.

Read the following passage from the Bible, then go back to the above list and ask yourself the suggested questions about what you've just read.

> "Praise be to the God and Father of our Lord Jesus Christ! In his great mercy he has given us new birth into a living hope through the resurrection of Jesus Christ from the dead, and into an inheritance that can never perish, spoil or fade—kept in heaven for you, who through faith are shielded by God's power until the coming of the salvation that is ready to be revealed in the last time. In this you greatly rejoice, though now for a little while you may have had to suffer grief in all kinds of trials.
>
> These have come so that your faith—of greater worth than gold, which perishes even though refined by fire—may be proved genuine and may result in praise, glory, and honor when Jesus Christ is revealed.
>
> Though you have not seen him, you love him; and even though you do not see him now, you believe in him and are filled with an inexpressible and glorious joy, for you are receiving the goal of your faith, the salvation of your souls."
> (1 Peter 1:3-9)

How did you do? Did answering the questions help you better remember and apply the passage? If so, plan to use these questions in your future Bible readings.

One of the usual effects of depression is an inability to concentrate and get things done. Simply by reading this book, you are fighting those tendencies already! Built into each day are **LifeFilters** to help you meditate on what you've just learned. We encourage you to do the same thing with the Bible, God's Word.

**Taking a daily dose of divine truth will go a long way toward helping you win the battle of depression.**

Again, please remember: the best weapon is useless if it is not employed. Take the *Weapon of Meditation* and begin opening God's Word. It *will* make a difference in your life. God promises it.

## KNOWLEDGE IS POWER

During the Christmas holidays of my internship year, our internal medicine team was short-handed. As an intern fresh out of medical school, I found myself responsible for dozens of critically ill patients. Ordinarily, I had the help of a half dozen medical students, a third-year "resident" who was two years ahead of me in my specialty, and an attending physician who was a professor in this field of medicine. But all of these members of the team were gone for Christmas vacation placing an extraordinary burden on the interns.

On the first Monday of the New Year, the students returned, along with our new staff physician. Our first order of business was grand rounds, a meeting where we reported the condition of our patients to our new overseeing attending physician.

As my fellow intern presented his first patient, it was obvious he had no idea of the cause of the man's disease. When the attending physician asked questions concerning lab results, X-ray reports, and therapy, the poor intern sputtered and shuffled his way through index cards without giving any real information. Quietly, the attending physician walked over to a window and pulled aside a curtain to gaze into the darkening evening sky. We looked at each other in puzzlement, until the intern worked up the nerve to ask what the physician was doing.

"It is obvious the only reason your patient has survived the Christmas holidays is because of miraculous divine intervention!" the doctor replied. "Therefore, my intrepid intern, I am looking for another star in the east."

You need to be more informed than this poor, overworked intern. So, today we are going to have Grand Rounds, and the subject is antidepressant medication. Please come into the conference room and let's join the attending physician on today's grand rounds. Remember, Knowledge is Power! Be prepared to ask those questions again!

*Sir, what about antidepressants? Where did they come from?*

Excellent question, my good student. At least you are showing more interest than our bewildered intern. During the 1960s, researchers trying to develop a cure for tuberculosis discovered a class of medication that did not affect the infection but elevated the mood of ill, depressed patients. By accident, the first antidepressants were developed. No star in the east this time, although I would not discount the intervention of the Great Physician.

*How do antidepressants work?*

I assume you have been on your field trip to the brain? Synapses and all of that, correct? Remember the gap and how neurotransmitters were needed to allow the spark to jump from one nerve cell to another? Antidepressant medications work by preventing the breakdown of these neurotransmitters we discussed previously, essentially increasing the levels of such chemicals like serotonin. Remember, these chemicals are necessary for the proper function of nerves, particularly my favorite neurotransmitter, serotonin.

*Sir, our intern, seems a bit depressed. How do you determine which medication to give?*

If we were to examine our intern closely, we would see he has his unique combination of symptoms. While all these medications are equally effective, some work better for different combinations of symptoms than others, if the first antidepressant you try does not provide sufficient relief, don't despair. Another probably will. Many depression sufferers must try several different medications before they find the one that works best for them.

*Can a patient expect immediate results?*

Taking an antidepressant can be frustrating in the short term. Most people experience some unpleasant side effects at first, while the benefits may take four to six weeks to appear.

**So, be patient.**

Not only will you be rewarded by the alleviation of symptoms with time, but the side effects will subside after a few weeks of using the medication. We now appreciate that antidepressant medications can lead to "neurogenesis" or growth and formation of new nerve connections, and this neurogenesis takes time.

*Sir, there are side effects?*

Ah, yes, side effects. In general, the antidepressant medication produces a host of similar side effects. These can include blurred vision, dry mouth, changes in sexual function, sleep disruption, drowsiness, and appetite changes. *However, not all of these drugs produce all of these side effects.* This is why it is so important to allow your physician to tailor the drug to your specific needs. Some side effects go away with time. Others do not and require changing your medication. In each case, your doctor and your pharmacist are ready to help you with the knowledge of your drug's side effects and the onset of effectiveness. And, let me add, I'm glad you're asking these questions. The more you know about the medication you may be taking, the more you can cope with any problems that may arise.

*How much and what type of antidepressant should we take?*

Different antidepressants have different effective dosages. It's important to note that the dose you take has *nothing* to do with the severity of your depression. Nor does the dose affect your hopes for recovery. The number of milligrams (mg) for an individual medication compared to another is irrelevant. Some antidepressants work at 15 mg a day, others at 200 mg a day. Don't compare apples and oranges.

**Recognizing this, be patient, as it often takes a while to get used to taking antidepressants.**

Most physicians start people on a low dose and slowly increase it over a few weeks or months. Again, having your dosage increased has nothing to do with the severity of your depression or your prognosis. It is a reflection of your individual response to the medication.

*Sir, can you get addicted to antidepressants?*

Good question. Patients need not fear addiction. Antidepressants are not addictive. And, the length of treatment is highly dependent on your individual response to therapy. Think of your medication as a diabetic thinks of insulin. You need it to function, and it carries no long-term effects.

*Sir, if I feel better, can I stop my medication?*

Never stop taking antidepressants abruptly. Let me say that again.

**NEVER stop taking antidepressants cold turkey!**

If you do, you may experience serious flu-like symptoms or even a worsening of your pre--existing depression. Your physician must taper you off the drug if you no longer need medical treatment. Now you see why I place so much emphasis on that relationship with your physician. Remember, you are in a partnership with your doctor to defeat your depression.

Well, that concludes our grand rounds for the day. You showed good attention today, and you asked many good questions. Remember, **Knowledge is Power,** and as you continue to add to the strength of your *Weapon of Knowledge*, you are more empowered than ever to defeat depression!

## LIFEFILTER #16

Today, I will:

- Partner with God to study His word on a daily basis.

- Partner with my physician to study the treatment options God has provided for my emotional health.

- Take a moment right now to stop and thank God for His love.

Scripture To Strengthen Me:

*"Study this Book of Instruction continually. Meditate on it day and night so you will be sure to obey everything written in it. Only then will you prosper and succeed in all you do." Joshua 1:8 (NLT)*

# 17

## DAY SEVENTEEN

# THE POWER TO CONQUER

At a critical point in the game, I noticed our players were tired. They were also beginning to make mistakes. If they continued playing the same way, the team would lose. I signaled for a timeout and called the players to the bench. Quickly, I told them to sit down and rest while I diagramed a different defense and some new plays. When the whistle blew to restart the game, the team was rested and had a plan to win. From there on, the game was ours.

I love sports. ESPN and I are old friends. So you might be wondering what kind of athletic team I coach.

I don't.

In the first paragraph, I wasn't talking about baseball, basketball, football, or any other type of team sport. Instead, I was talking about the biggest game of all: *life*! The players could have been a husband and wife at a difficult time in their marriage. Or it could have been a couple struggling with the debilitating effects of depression and unhappiness.

Are you someone who believes talking to a counselor is unneeded? If so, think of a counselor as a "coach." Does that sound far-fetched? In any game, the players are so involved on the field or court that they are often unable to see how the flow of play is developing. They may have begun "grooving in" some bad habits that will hinder them. Or, they may simply be tired. A good coach watches carefully from the sidelines and understands the players' problems. When he or she spots a weakness, the coach quickly calls a timeout and allows the team some time to rest while getting them back on the right track.

Good counselors do the same thing. They can see, from the sidelines, the flow of your life. Unbiased, they can give you both time to rest and good advice on how to get your life back on track. Because they have seen a lot of "teams" and watched a lot of "games," their experience can guide you and help you avoid the same mistakes others have made.

**In short, a good counselor can help you win the game of life.**

There's another good reason for using a counselor: the Bible recommends it! Let's take a look at several scriptures, beginning with a description of Jesus Christ:

> *"For to us, a child is born, to us, a son is given, and the government will be on his shoulders. And he will be called* **Wonderful Counselor,** *Mighty God, Everlasting Father, Prince of Peace." (Isaiah 9:6, emphasis added)*

Yes, Jesus Christ, Himself, is the greatest counselor of all! His wisdom and insight into life are revealed to us in the Bible. The more we read it, meditate on it and absorb it, the better we will be able to handle all that life throws at us.

But God says He has given us others to help us, as well.

One of our allies is the local church. Our Heavenly Father has decreed that we find other brothers and sisters in Christ and develop meaningful relationships with them. Together, we help one another, and together, we worship God.

Part of developing meaningful relationships with other Christians is being willing to share problems and doubts with them. Again, as I've said once before, be careful with whom you share. Make sure they are positive, mature Christians who can take what you say, continue to love you, and give you the benefit of their wisdom. **But do share.** The Christians I've just described are out there – and God has given them some wonderful abilities to help people just like you.

*"Bear one another's burdens, and so fulfill the law of Christ." (Galatians 6:2 NKJV)*

In other words, as you share your problems, doubts, and burdens, you not only allow other Christians to use the gifts God has given them, you also *allow them to fulfill the law of Christ!* And remember:

**They can't bear if you don't share.**

Finally, God gives some people a very unique ability to "read" people and help them with their lives. Jesus Christ, Wonderful Counselor, has also given earthly counselors to help us through the difficult passages of life. Look at what God's Word has to say about them and your own life:

*"Where there is no counsel, the people fall; But in the multitude of counselors there is safety." (Proverbs 11:14 NKJV)*
*"Without counsel, plans go awry, But in the multitude of counselors they are established." (Proverbs 15:22 NKJV)*

According to God, trying to make it through this world

alone is to be doomed to failure. Without counselors, people can fall morally and spiritually. Without wise counsel, your plans in life can fail. God has given you His Son, Jesus Christ, as the ultimate Counselor. He has given you the local church, with some wise Christians in it, to help you in your daily walk. And He has gifted some people as counselors to help you with, especially difficult times.

*Don't turn away from any gift of help God offers you!* If you need help with your depression or unhappiness, let someone gifted in the area of counseling use their gift to help you move back into the light. Make today the day you leave your solitude behind.

## KNOWLEDGE IS POWER

I sat in my car, watching my windows frost over from the cool November air. Across the street, the house sat nestled among trees whose fiery red leaves were giving way to the inevitability of autumn. The house had two stories and a huge front porch built in the days when sitting outside and visiting with neighbors was a vital part of everyday life. I watched a porch swing move gently in the fall breeze and saw movement through the large windows. If I didn't know better, I could imagine a family going about their normal evening routine, sitting in front of the fireplace; talking about the events of the day; anticipating the promise of the future. I knew this was not the case. For, within this house dwelled endless pain.

With growing terror and trepidation, I stepped out of my car, drew a deep breath, and took the first step in a journey that would change my life forever. Inside the warm living room, a smiling woman greeted me from behind a sliding glass window.

"I'm Doctor . . ." I paused, feeling vulnerable and conspicuous. I glanced around at the young couple sitting nervously on the couch. On the love seat, an older woman dabbed at her nose with a tissue, staring off into the unknowable distance. This place was the great equalizer. Here, titles and degrees and social stature meant nothing. Here we were all struggling for answers to our individual problems. I gave my name to the woman and sat stiffly in the corner, ready to bolt out of the room any minute. I didn't need to be here! I didn't need this kind of help! All I needed was some time, and I could handle these problems on my own. There wasn't anything wrong with me. I wasn't crazy!

My thoughts were interrupted by a smiling man. His bright blue eyes were alive with energy, and his smile was genuine. He motioned me up the stairs, and I climbed out of my old world into a new one.

It took years of concerted pleading on my wife's part to make me finally go to the counselor. But, in the two years that followed, I never regretted making that first climb up the stairs.

Is professional counseling an option for you? Should you talk to someone? Absolutely. Without question. No doubt about it.

Who, then, should you talk to? You may be puzzled by all the choices. I want to help you understand the array of possibilities available to you and the professionals involved in the process of counseling.

A **psychiatrist** is a medical doctor and can write prescriptions, overseeing the medical aspects of mental health. After graduating from medical school, a psychiatrist will go through a three-year residency program in psychiatry. For those illnesses requiring hospitalization, the psychiatrist heads up a team of workers who join together to help the patient through his or her illness. Patients may need a psychiatrist in the early stages of a major depressive disorder.

A **psychologist** has a master's degree or a bachelor of science degree in psychology. Sometimes, a psychologist will pursue a Ph.D. in psychology and will be referred to as a doctor.

Psychologists are trained in methods of behavioral therapy or psychotherapy. They do not write prescriptions and do not oversee the medical problems of their patients but focus on behavioral treatment.

Professional counselors, such as pastors, have special training in counseling and exposure to the principles of behavioral therapy. They may form the first line of help. When they see the severity of a depressive episode, they may refer the client on to a psychologist or psychiatrist.

**Where do you start?**

- If you are a member of a church, start with your pastor and ask him to recommend a consultation with a professional with counseling expertise. Your church may have a *certified*, trained counselor as a staff member.
- You may choose a counseling center. Counseling centers use professional counselors or psychologists, and some counseling centers have a foundation in Christian counseling.
- If you have seen your physician, he may advise a course of therapy and refer you to a counselor or psychologist.
- If you are thinking of harming yourself, then you should go immediately to the nearest hospital emergency room.

**What then can you expect from your counseling session?**

The most commonly used technique is cognitive-behavioral therapy (CBT). "Cognitive" refers to thought processes. Cognitive therapy is a powerful self-help technique for dealing with depression and other negative emotions by *consciously changing the way we think*. The premise is that your moods are directly related to your thinking pattern.

Negative thoughts affect your sense of self and can also influence your behavior and even your physical state. A CBT focused therapist helps you to recognize distorted, self-critical thoughts, and once you recognize the assumptions behind those thoughts, leads you to correct them by changing your perspective.

With more profound levels of depression, you may have to resort to interpersonal psychotherapy that concentrates more on current relationships. Psychodynamic therapy is even more intensive and focuses on how life events, desires, and relationships affect your feelings and the choices you make.

Don't worry about these confusing names. The point of this discussion is to illustrate the wide variety of therapies available depending on your level of depression and your unique life circumstances. However, it is not up to US to decide our therapy. Your therapist will know in which direction to move you for the best and quickest results.

**What are the benefits of seeking professional counseling?**

**First**, the counselor, in most cases, does not know you. You can share anything on your mind without fear of being judged.

**Second**, the counselor is trained in techniques to determine when you are not truthful with yourself. The counselor holds up a mirror to your behavior to help you become aware of your own behavior patterns.

**Third**, the counselor is there to help you. He or she is not there to ridicule you or condemn you. You are paying them to help you. That is their job. For the hour you are sitting in their office, the counselor's whole reason for existence is to help you and you alone. No distractions. No hidden agendas. No fear of rejection.

**Fourth,** the counselor is unbiased in their ability to appraise your behavior. They can ask telling questions that make you think about your behavior in a totally new light. Gaining a different perspective on your pattern of thinking and behavior is the basis for overcoming depression.

After two years of counseling, I walked away from that antebellum home a different person. And, the counseling stuck. I internalized the changes. Before I went to counseling, depression was a constant companion, striking without warning and crippling me for days as I struggled to overcome it.

**During the two years of counseling, I learned to recognize the trigger events in my life that brought on bouts of depression.**

I saw the train coming before it hit me. Now, after four years, I've learned to stay off the tracks. Depression still haunts me, but it's infrequent. And when it comes, I have a step-by-step method for dealing with depression and overcoming it.

**Depression no longer controls my life. And you can keep it from controlling your life, as well.**

Let me pause for a second and talk to the men reading this book. There is no mystery that we want to fix things ourselves. *We don't need no stinking counselor!* The truth is, **we do.** And, the sooner you decide to get help, the quicker you will begin to overcome depression.

One of my dear friends fell into a profound depression. When I suggested counseling, he just shrugged. His depression was so bad; he stopped playing golf. Trust me, his greatest love in life outside his family was golf! For him to quit the game was very telling!

I knew something about his golf game. He paid a golf coach every week to improve his game. I pointed out a simple fact. Why would he pay hundreds of dollars a month to improve his golf game, but not be willing to go to a "depression coach," a counselor, to help overcome his depression?

Don't wait for YEARS like I did while my wife begged me to get help. Take it from another man who has been through the counseling and has come out of the valley of the shadow of death.

**GO GET HELP TODAY!**

Make a decision today to seek professional counseling, if you haven't already. Your *Weapon of Knowledge* today is: Don't waste years of needless misery because you are too proud to admit you need help. It will be the best walk up the stairs you've ever had.

# LIFEFILTER #17

Today, I will:

- Remember: God does not want me to be alone in this world. That's why He is *always* with me.

- Resolve: To leave isolation and share meaningfully with some positive, wise Christians.

- I will pray about finding a godly counselor and letting him/her partner with me in overcoming depression.

Scripture To Strengthen Me:

"Make this your common practice: Confess your sins to each other and pray for each other so that you can live together whole and healed. The prayer of a person living right with God is something powerful to be reckoned with." James 5:16 (The Message)

# 18

## DAY EIGHTEEN

# THE POWER TO CONQUER

A persistent cough decided to settle in my chest this past winter. When I wanted to talk, I either constantly kept a cough drop in my mouth, or I hacked and wheezed. As you can imagine, it wasn't a pretty sight. My physician recommended and prescribed several high-powered medicines: steroids, antibiotics, and a variety of cough medicines. One of those was a decongestant. As you probably know, the main function of a decongestant is to thin out – water down, if you will – the thick mucus causing the cough and congestion. As this substance is diluted, the lungs are then better able to expel the invader and breathe more clearly.

Using that analogy, we could say that today's medicine for depression is a decongestant. It dilutes your depression, helping you expel it from your mind and body. If I could use another analogy, I would also call this a "syrup." I don't know about you, but I've never found a cough syrup that tastes good. When I have to take a dose, I hold my nose, grimace, and swallow the stuff. I hate the taste, but I take it anyway because I know it's good for me.

**When you are depressed, there is a great temptation to pull yourself into a shell and stay away from everyone.**

In this dark hole, alone, you concentrate on your problems and magnify your inadequacies. Before long, your situation seems so bad, and you feel so unworthy of anything good, that you are pummeled about by the torrent of guilt rushing over you. Bewildered, you sink ever deeper into the black hole your depression has created. Retreating, you become more and more isolated from everyone. You find yourself surrounded by a suffocating, ever-thickening swamp of negativity.

Did I overstate your situation? Probably not. In any case, I want to paint as realistic a picture as possible. *I want you to see that left to itself, your depression will grow stronger.* As it thickens, this invader clogs the pathways of your emotions and tries to bring all rational thought to a sluggish stop.

It's time for what I call the "Syrup of Communication." And, I'm sorry to say, it's a lot like the cough syrups I described earlier. For many of us, it won't taste good. That's because our depression makes us want to stay isolated. It's hard for us to reach up out of our dark hole and try to communicate with others. But just like the syrup with the bad taste, go ahead and take the medication, no matter how difficult it may be. This is one medicine that works!

An amazing transformation begins to take place when you allow communication with others to enter your life. As you share your thoughts, guilt, and anxieties with others, your depression begins to thin out. Diluted, it is then easier to deal with.

Communication, of course, is a two-way street. Both the act of sharing and the act of listening help you gain perspective. Here are three powerful results that will help you overcome your depression:

1. Reaching out to someone else forces you out of your hole of isolation.
2. Airing your fears robs them of much of their power.
3. Exposing them to the light of day makes them pale and less significant.

As you prepare to do this, however, I must caution you to be on your guard.

**Your emotions may very well begin screaming at you to stay apart from everyone.**

Your flight reflex may be on full alert, ready to pull you back from the first hint of meaningful communication. You can overcome this by reminding yourself that depression causes your emotions to paint a false picture. Instead, hold your nose and grimace all you want, but take the "Syrup of Communication" and begin to get better.

One question that needs to be answered is: With whom should you communicate? First of all, it is *imperative that it be a godly person*. In this instance, you need someone who is wise, positive, encouraging, and who cares about you. It may be a close friend; in my life, my wife fills this role wonderfully. It might also be a Christian counselor or a church staff member who is gifted in this area. **However, above all, don't stay isolated.**

Finally, make sure you communicate with God. As you reach out of your isolation to Him, you will find a nail-scarred hand already reaching out toward you to give understanding, love, and strength. Perhaps the words of David express how you feel:

*"Listen to my prayer, O God, do not ignore my plea; hear me*

*and answer me. My thoughts trouble me, and I am distraught." (Psalm 55:1-2)*

Do you feel like this? Evidently, you're not alone. David was Israel's greatest king and the composer of more psalms than any other person, but even he had times of emotional difficulty. As the psalm suggests, however, David did not stay isolated. Instead, he poured out his heart to God. In doing so, he learned an important lesson -- and he has passed it on to you in this paraphrase:

*"Trust in him at all times, dear reader; pour out your heart to him, for God is your refuge." (Psalm 62:8)*

God is your refuge. He wants to listen to you. Communicate with Him today – and with those around you as well. As you do, you'll find your depression diluted, your mood lifted, and your emotions strengthened.

# KNOWLEDGE IS POWER

In the 21$^{st}$ century, society has tried to blur the lines between masculine and feminine. We live in such a politically correct culture we try to downplay the differences between men and women. The reality is that men and women are very, very different, physically, psychologically, and emotionally. We must understand how depression affects each gender. And, for those of the opposite gender in your life, YOU need to understand how differently depression affects them. To that end, today will feature two sections, one for women and one for men. I will leave it up to you as to which section to read! Ladies first!

## WOMEN

Fact: more women than men are likely to be diagnosed with depression. Why? The answer to that question is the subject of much research into the biological, social, and psychological factors that are unique to women. Instead of going into an exhaustive exploration of these factors, I want to focus on two topics: fibromyalgia and hormonal influences.

**Fibromyalgia**

My sister began to suffer from great pain in her chest. Alarmed that she might be having heart problems, she asked for my help, and I referred her to a cardiologist. It turned out that her heart was fine. What now? She began having pain in her joints and her muscles. I recommended a rheumatologist, a doctor specializing in arthritis. His diagnosis was immediate. My sister was under enormous stress caring for our ailing mother. She was suffering from fibromyalgia.

For decades, the diagnosis of fibromyalgia was considered a myth. In fact, old school physicians still think fibromyalgia is not a real disease. Women suffer from this malady almost exclusively over men. And, now research has shown there is a definite link between depression and the chronic type of pain of fibromyalgia.

Fibromyalgia causes chronic, widespread muscle pain, tiredness, and multiple tender points – not just muscles but also joints. I will talk more about the relationship between chronic pain and depression shortly. But, for now, I want to reassure women that there is a biological, chemical reason women suffer from pain in fibromyalgia and develop depression.

What we have discovered is that *depression can produce certain chemicals in the body that trigger pain by promoting inflammation*. Did you read that? There is a chemical surging through your body that is causing pain because it promotes inflammation. And, the signs of inflammation are pain, swelling, redness, heat, and sometimes loss of function. Treating depression can help women overcome chronic pain and fibromyalgia. The two appear to be tightly connected. If you suffer from fibromyalgia, you are dealing with the result of depression or severe stress. Once again, you will need to consult with a physician to attack both the pain and tenderness and the underlying depression and stress. But, there is hope for any woman suffering from these symptoms.

**Hormones**

After surviving the last three years of alternating freezing temperatures and arid conditions in my own house, I can tell you without a doubt that my wife is far too familiar with the effects of "female hormones." Hormones have a direct effect on the brain chemistry that controls emotions and mood. When do these hormones affect women's brains? Puberty. During menstrual periods. Before – During – After pregnancy. Menopause. Ladies, you don't get a break! Let's look at three specific examples of how hormones produce depression.

**Premenstrual dysphoric disorder** is a mouthful. PMDD is a severe form of premenstrual syndrome leading to depression, anxiety, irritability, and mood swings the week before menstruation. PMDD is not necessarily due to unusual hormone changes but may be related to a woman having a different response to these hormonal changes.

**Postpartum depression** is well known. After giving birth, some women experience depression from the hormonal and physical changes along with the responsibility of caring for a newborn. It is important to understand that postpartum depression is far more serious than just the "baby blues." Women or their significant other must be able to recognize when depression is more severe than expected. Fortunately, follow up visits to the doctor help in recognition of this devastating form of depression.

**Menopause** may not lead to depression. But, some women may transition into menopause with a high risk for depression. Fortunately, depression becomes less common for women during the post-menopause period.

While we haven't discussed treatment for these hormone-related episodes of depression, the take away from this section is this: **Women are at a much higher risk for depression** because of the fluctuation in female hormones. Be aware of this, women. (And, men!) If you are depressed, discuss with your doctor the possibility that your hormones may be responsible and see if supplemental hormonal therapy might help with the fluctuations in brain chemistry.

Your *Weapon of Knowledge* ladies is this: Realize there are very specific, unique aspects of depression that can occur in women only.

**Be aware of the reality of chronic pain and fibromyalgia as it most likely indicates an underlying degree of extreme mental stress or depression.**

And understand the influence of hormonal changes on your behavior. Be prepared to get professional help! Don't suffer alone!

**MEN**

Okay, guys, it's our turn. Yeah, I know we don't want to think about depression, much less talk about it. But, it is a silent killer among men. So, like it or not, you got to deal with it! So, let's deal with it!

**Inconvenient fact #1: Depression is harder to recognize in men.**

I love to eat. At lunch, I think about what I am going to eat at supper (that's the designation for dinner down here in the South). I can look back on my life before I admitted I suffered from depression and use my weight gains as signposts that I was depressed and didn't admit it.

As men, we have to be strong and in control of our emotions at all times. When we feel hopeless, helpless, or overwhelmed by despair, we tend to deny it. Instead of acting all weepy and "down," we express our depression in other ways. We drink too much. We eat too much. We use drugs. So, for us guys, here is a checklist of possible symptoms of our depression:

- Fatigue
- Sleep Problems
- Stomachache or backache
- Irritability
- Difficulty concentrating
- Anger or hostility
- Substance abuse
- Sexual dysfunction
- Indecision

Now, before you get all upset, realize that any one of these symptoms can exist alone and not be related to underlying depression. But, if you are experiencing over **half** of these symptoms, you might be depressed.

Guys, let me be very direct and a bit repetitive because sometimes we need to be knocked in the head to get it.

**More than 5 *million* men in the U.S. experience depression each year.**

Depression in men can often be overlooked, as many of us find it difficult to talk about our feelings. Instead, we tend to focus on the physical symptoms that often accompany depression, such as back pain, headaches, difficulty sleeping, or sexual problems. This can result in the underlying depression going untreated, which can have serious consequences.

In fact, men suffering from depression are **four** times more likely to commit suicide than women. It's important for any man to seek help with depression before feelings of despair become feelings of suicide. You need to talk honestly with a friend, loved one, or doctor about what's going on in your mind as well as your body. Once correctly diagnosed, there is plenty you can do to successfully treat and manage depression.

**Inconvenient Fact #2: The causes of depression in men are different than in women.**

Recent research has focused on the role of stress in producing depression in men. Rather than having a low level of such neurotransmitters such as serotonin, stress continuously puts the neurons in an "on" position. It is important to understand that the cause of depression in a man may be different from the cause of depression in a woman. And, this means a man may need a different approach in treatment, not only from a counseling point of view but also from a medication point of view.

**Inconvenient Fact #3: A depressed man can seldom get well on his own.**

We MUST GET HELP! Let me say that again. GO GET PROFESSIONAL HELP! Remember my colleague who loved golf? If you are consistently slicing with that three iron, you pay a golf coach to help you with your swing. Isn't it worth the money to cut a few extra strokes from your golf game? IF YOU ARE WILLING TO SEEK HELP FOR YOUR GOLF SWING, WHY DON'T YOU SEEK HELP FOR YOUR DEPRESSION!

> **Seven out of ten depressed men will never seek professional help.**

This is probably the main cause of the high suicide rate among men.

However, of the men who do seek relief, 85% report satisfaction with gaining relief from their depressive symptoms.

Did you get that last statement? Read it again. If you seek professional help, let's say from a depression coach, I mean, a counselor, then there is an 85% chance you can conquer your depression. I don't think those kinds of statistics are as good for your golf swing!

**Your *Weapon of Knowledge* today is this: Men suffer from depression almost as frequently as women, and we need to recognize it and get help!**

I know that it is an inconvenient fact, but it is true. And, to deny this is to buy into the lie that we are too strong ever to be depressed. Let me remind you once again to ask the question, "What is the lie?" The lie is that you can never really be depressed. The truth is you can get depressed and probably are depressed. Remember, Satan is the father of lies. God is truth! Listen to the truth and admit your problems and get help!

**Teenagers and Young Adults**
I'm writing this section in 2019. In their book, "*So the Next Generation Will Know,*" Sean McDowell and J. Warner Wallace give a portrait of "Generation Z." This generation of young people are "digital natives." As I mentioned earlier, they have grown up "online,", and we have to teach them how to be "offline." They are researchers.

Remember the chapter on information overload? This generation is one quick keystroke away from any and all knowledge. Google is their new god. They are visual multitaskers focusing on visual platforms often many at one time. With all of this in mind, they are impatient! Speed and convenience rule the day. Answers are literally at their fingertips. Average attention span? 8 seconds!

These young people are racially diverse and also very fluid, "blurring the lines between work and home, truth and fiction, fact and feeling, and our public and private lives." They are social justice-oriented, focusing on causes surrounding human equality. They are ultimately pragmatic and are worried about the future.

And here is the heart of understanding why this generation now has the highest suicide rate ever in the history of America. They are overwhelmed! With social media, these young people find it increasingly difficult to escape their troubles. Their biggest fear. FOMO. Fear Of Missing Out!

**And, ultimately, they are lonely! Experts now believe this generation is on the verge of the greatest mental health crisis in decades.**

Why? The presence of smartphones and other forms of social media have created an unprecedented situation in which these young people do not know how to have personal interaction!

And, finally, they are "post-Christian." Our culture has created such an open, agenda led attack against Christianity that this "worldview" is no longer viewed with a positive attitude. In fact, most young people today find themselves not "atheists" but "apatheists." The "nones" are the largest growing group in our society; those who have no interest in any type of religious affiliation.

In summary, every factor we have discussed so far contributing to depression is exponentially multiplied in the lives of young people! However, if you are a young person reading this, we are going to give you help to deal with these forces you are facing every day. There is hope ahead.

## LIFEFILTER #18

Today, I will:

- Talk to God, because I *know* that He hears me.

- Seek out godly persons with whom I can share.

- Go back and read 2 Corinthians 1:4 again. I will try to fulfill this verse on a regular basis.

Scripture To Strengthen Me:

"Praise God, the Father of our Lord Jesus Christ! The Father is a merciful God, who always gives us comfort. He comforts us when we are in trouble, so that we can share that same comfort with others in trouble." 2 Corinthians 1:3–4 (CEV)

# 19

## DAY NINETEEN

# THE POWER TO CONQUER

The first Sunday church service had just concluded, with a second one getting ready to start. Hundreds of people swirled around me, laughing, talking with one another, catching up with friends on what had happened in the last week. Many from the first service stopped and thanked me for my sermon as they made their way to Bible Study.

I watched as an elderly woman shuffled slowly toward where I stood. As she got closer, I reached down toward her. She let go of her walker and gave me a long, fierce hug. Then, giving a small smile, she whispered, "Thanks, Pastor. Thanks." In response, I gave her one more "bonus" hug.

Why do I tell you this story? Because I know how important moments such as these were to this woman. Several weeks before, she had confided an important piece of information: my hug was the only friendly touch she received all week! Sure, she listened to the sermon, enjoyed the music, and participated in the Bible studies. But, a meaningful touch was missing in the midst of all of this. I gladly provided that hug every week!

"Touch" is a powerful medicine. Something wonderful happens when one person touches another in love and compassion. It's like a gentle electric current flowing back and forth, affecting both individuals for the better.

Some people are more comfortable with physical contact than are others. If you look at my background, for example, you'll see I grew up in a family that hugged and kissed one another regularly. In addition, I have an outgoing personality. If I'm around you for awhile and you look like you're sad or depressed, I'll probably try to give you a warm hug. If I see you're uncomfortable with that, I'll at least pat you on the shoulder.

In our house, Donna and I regularly give each other hugs and pats. We hold hands all the time. People say to us, "We think it's wonderful the two of you still show you're in love." And often I'll respond by saying, "Things like this are what have kept us close over the years."

I've given you this background on myself so that you can understand the import of this next statement. *When I'm depressed, I don't want anyone to come near me, touch me, try to hug me or do anything that I would have to respond to.* What has happened to change me so much? I've been infected with the disease of depression. One of its symptoms is a creeping paralysis which, if left unchecked, will infiltrate every part of my body.

One of the cures for this is to liberally apply the medicine of touch.

Again, I don't want to touch or be touched. But intellectually I know I must go against my emotions.

Let me remind you that, together, we have learned over the past several days of this book that all of us have the power to choose to act against our emotions. So I allow my wife to embrace me, and I make sure I hug back. Of course, Donna is a nurse, and she's as smart as a whip. Knowing the power of depression, she won't let me go with just one hug. Instead, she will hug me many times more than normal if she sees the numbing flow of depression wash over me.

During His earthly ministry, Jesus knew about the tremendous, transferable power of touch. As you read these next words, try to identify with the woman at the heart of this vivid event from the life of Christ:

> *A large crowd followed and pressed around him (Jesus). And a woman was there who had been subject to bleeding for twelve years. She had suffered a great deal under the care of many doctors and had spent all she had, yet instead of getting better she grew worse. When she heard about Jesus, she came up behind him in the crowd and **touched** his cloak, because she thought, "If I just **touch** his clothes, I will be healed." Immediately her bleeding stopped and she felt in her body that she was freed from her suffering.*
>
> *At once Jesus realized that power had gone out from him. He turned around in the crowd and asked, "Who **touched** my clothes?"*
>
> *"You see the people crowding against you," his disciples answered, "and yet you can ask, 'Who **touched** me?'"*
>
> *But Jesus kept looking around to see who had done it. Then the woman, knowing what had happened to her, came and fell at his feet and, trembling with fear, told him the whole truth. He said to her, "Daughter, your faith has healed you. Go in peace and be freed from your suffering." (Mark 5:24-34, emphasis added)*

The transferable power of touch. Jesus used it frequently in His dealings with those who were ill.

Jesus touched the blind:

> *"'Lord,' they answered, 'we want our sight.' Jesus had compassion on them and **touched** their eyes. Immediately*

*they received their sight and followed him." (Matthew 20:33-34, emphasis added)*

Jesus touched those who could not hear or speak:

- *"There some people brought to him a man who was deaf and could hardly talk, and they begged him to place his hand on the man. After he took him aside, away from the crowd, Jesus put his fingers into the man's ears. Then he spit and **touched** the man's tongue. He looked up to heaven and with a deep sigh said to him, 'Ephphatha!' (which means, 'Be opened!'). At this, the man's ears were opened, his tongue was loosened and e began to speak plainly." (Mark 7:32-35, emphasis added)*

Jesus even touched those who were repulsive to society:

*"While Jesus was in one of the towns, a man came along who was covered with leprosy. When he saw Jesus, he fell with his face to the ground and begged him, 'Lord, if you are willing, you can make me clean.' Jesus reached out his hand and **touched** the man. 'I am willing,' he said. 'Be clean!' And immediately the leprosy left him." (Luke 5:12-13, emphasis added)*

Why did Jesus insist on touching all of these people? After all, He could have healed any one of them by simply speaking His will. I believe it's because our Savior, who knows the heart of His children better than anyone, knew these deprived men and women needed to be healed in more ways than one. When Christ healed them, He did so completely. The blind, deaf, and lame not only became whole physically, but Christ also forgave them of their sins and strengthened their emotions. *His touch was a powerful part of helping them emotionally.*

A mighty warhorse on his way to battle was stopped by the sight of a sparrow in the middle of the road. Flat on its back, its tiny claws pointed toward the sky, the bird made an unusual sight.

"What in the world are you doing?" the war horse asked.

"Oh, mighty warrior," replied the sparrow, "this morning, I heard the sky was going to fall."

The horse gave a derisive snort. "Do you really think your pitiful legs are going to make any difference in the outcome?"

Said the sparrow wisely, "One does what one can." [11]

**That is all God asks of you and me: to do what we can. The surprising element in all of this is that when we do what we can with what we have, God blesses in amazing ways.**

Sometimes, to our astonishment, wonderful things are accomplished.

The next time depression begins infecting you, take your medicine: find someone to hug and touch. You may not believe it at the time, but that touch will eventually help heal you of the numbness which holds you fast.

John L. Mason once said, "The best helping hand you will ever find is at the end of your own arm." [12] Use it to touch others and, in the process, heal yourself.

# KNOWLEDGE IS POWER

Today I want to introduce four important strategies for conquering depression. These four strategies will help you reverse the effects of habits and behaviors in your life that have led you into depression.

**The first strategy is: Turn Off the Tech!**

Beth has over 1,500 friends. She talks to six of her friends a dozen times every day. Every night she plays games with four or her friends. However, Beth never leaves her room. In fact, she never leaves her house! While Beth claims she is surrounded by friends, the fact is, she is totally alone!

Fact #1: **We are now more connected than ever. And yet, we are now more alone than ever!**

Tyler just finished the last level in one of the most popular first-person shooter games just released four days ago. He is exultant and triumphant! He has saved the galaxy. But, when Tyler leaves his game room to take a shower for the first time in four days and to get ready to sleep for the first time in four days, he notices an alien crouching in his bathroom. He reaches for his imaginary gun because his world of fantasy has just crossed over into his world of reality.

**Fact #2: People immersed in the virtual world often experience the "Tetris Effect" where elements of their fantasy world intrude into their perception of the real world – the boundaries between virtual and real are now blurred!**

Sam is stuck in traffic and desperately wants to get home. He wants to see his family, but he also wants to get online with one of his college buddies and play a video game. In the video game, he has almost advanced to the highest level by becoming an aggressive driver of fast cars. Suddenly, he finds himself honking his horn, screaming at the car in front of him and revving his engine. Why don't these fools get out of the way? Two minutes later, Sam's aggressive driving style backfires, and he rams into the car in front of him, causing a major traffic pileup.

**Fact #3: Violent video games and violent media produce changes in behavior and make you more aggressive and more violent! This leads to depression. Ideas have consequences!**

I have discussed this topic earlier, but I want to revisit the idea that our immersive, information-rich, technologically advanced society is burning out our brains. Is there proof of this? Or, is this concept just an old school reaction to new technology?

Scientific research in this area is very active. Numerous studies over the past twenty years have tried to address the effects of information overload on the human brain, primarily in the areas of video gaming addiction, violent media, and violent video games. While there are many detractors to this premise, use common sense. If ideas did not have consequences, then how would advertising work? If exposure to certain concepts did not produce permanent changes in behavior, then why have education? Most importantly, if the most dangerous idea in the history of humanity could not produce changes in behavior, then why crucify Jesus of Nazareth?

**Basically, many studies have substantiated the fact that prolonged exposure to immersive digital content without rest or sleep depletes those precious neurotransmitters I mentioned earlier.**

Once these neurotransmitter levels fall and remain low, you become depressed.

Scientific studies have revealed that prolonged contact with the internet, specifically online gaming, can lead to addiction and eventually can cause "rewiring" of structures in the brain.[13]

**Virtual reality alters brain reality!**

In Sean McDowell's book, "So The Next Generation Will Know," he notes that the younger generation is experiencing a dramatic increase in the levels of depression and loneliness. This is attributed to one thing: the smartphone! The prevalence of smartphones in this generation and their total reliance on that type of interaction have created an entire generation more lonely than ever in the history of America. Why? Because they have lost the ability to have person to person interaction.

Your *Weapon of Knowledge* for today is Strategy #1: **TURN OFF THE TECH!**

Start slow. Take a five-minute break every hour. Put aside the texting, emailing, social media, laptop, desktop, tablet, or the smartphone. It will be VERY difficult. We are addicted to digital tech. It is as important to us today as the party line was to the family in the 1950s. Try to build up to an hour a day away from technology. Read a book (yes, e-book readers are okay as long as you don't surf the internet while you're reading), go to a movie, go outside for a walk without your iPod! Then work yourself up to an entire weekend without tech. You will be amazed at the freedom you feel. But, it will be hard, and you may become anxious. However, the rewards will be great. Here is what my twenty-something son, Sean, had to say about giving up video gaming that would keep him up until the wee hours of every morning:

*I've played video games for most of my life. Some of my fondest memories from childhood involve gaming with friends. I still know my way around the first Zelda game instinctively. I have no memory of learning what comes naturally to me with games - playing them well is like riding a bike. I love good stories told well in any medium, and I love the interactive experiences that only gaming can provide.*

*I hate what gaming has become. I hate that gaming has become an executive's market, making lowest-denominator products for the easiest possible market. I am weary of gaming because gaming has stopped asking the hard questions. And for gaming, that means the default setting is realistic, and the default verb is "kill."*

*I am troubled that this shift also reflects something about our culture. When we lose touch with Christ our Peace, the Prince of Peace whose Kingdom comes in peace, we tend to elevate self above all else - entitlement (both to things unearned and to holding on tightly to what we are stewards of), pride, even patriotism - these can all take His place. And when what we love is not freely given to us, we default to violence as a way to protect what we have and take what we want.*

*A culture of self brings us out of balance with the Lord and with each other. His kingdom comes in peace, and anything that brings us* out of balance with that peace lends towards entropy, violence, and chaos. We have a longing for family, for home, for permanence in who we love and what we love to do, and when we elevate those things above the God who provides them, they only amplify (rather than relieve) our pain and anger.

When we don't hold to Christ, the Giver of all good things, we jealously and violently defend what we love because we feel we have no choice, because we feel entitled. That form of nihilism will eventually and inevitably lead towards our death.

Your *Weapon of Knowledge* today is found in Strategy #1: Turn Off the Tech! Take a vacation from the digital world into the real world and let your brain find rest!

# LIFEFILTER #19

Today, I will:

- Thank God for reaching out and touching me through His Son.

- Take a break from the digital world and step into the real world.

Scripture To Strengthen Me:

*"A man with leprosy came and knelt before him and said, 'Lord, if you are willing, you can make me clean.' Jesus reached out his hand and touched the man. 'I am willing,' he said. 'Be clean!' Immediately he was cleansed of his leprosy." Matthew 8:2–3*

**20**
---

**DAY TWENTY**

# THE POWER TO CONQUER

Safety. God wants to inject this wonderful quality into your life, beginning today. Here's how it can happen....

Pulling into the fast-food restaurant, I saw something unusual. Five telephone repair trucks dotted the parking lot. Either Hardee's was experiencing major telephone difficulties, or the drivers had decided to take a coffee break together. But what caught my attention were the bright orange cones -- the kind usually seen at highway construction sites -- sitting behind each truck. The men could not have backed out without crushing them.

Inside the restaurant, the men were sitting around a small table, talking and laughing. I ordered my food; on the way past their table, curiosity finally got the best of me.

"Excuse me," I said, stopping beside them. "Would you tell me why the cones are behind your trucks?"

One of the men laughed and said, "'Cause we'd get fired if we didn't. It's the rule." Then he added, "Seriously, we can't see very well behind these trucks. Putting the cone directly in our path every time we park forces us to look before we back out."

Another repairman broke in. "Several weeks ago, one of our

men was driving a truck that carries the big buckets. He had stopped for lunch and put out one of the cones. When it was time to leave, he walked to the back to pick it up. Right beside the cone, under the left rear wheel, was a small boy who had gotten away from his mother just a few seconds before."

The man shook his head. "If that guy hadn't had a cone behind his truck...."

The men finished their coffee, waved to the waitresses, and returned to their trucks. Each went to the rear of his vehicle, looked underneath it, and picked up the orange cone.

Safety. Always.

Where are the orange cones in your life? God has placed them in some specific areas. He wants to keep you from running over that which is sensitive and vulnerable in your heart and soul. Often, however, we decide to take matters into our own hands and begin moving – or even taking away – God's safety barriers. When that occurs, our direction in life, our relationships, and our priorities slip out of control.

**It's ironic, but the more we try to control our life instead of letting God have the reins, the more our life careens wildly about, unmanageable and dangerous to us.**

That's one of the reasons Jesus said:

*"For whoever wants to save his life will lose it, but whoever loses his life for me will save it." (Luke 9:24)*

God is the Master Designer. He knows everything there is to know about our bodies, minds, and emotions. He knows things about us science has not yet even dreamed of. So it stands to reason that we should abandon control of our life, giving it totally to the One who loves us. In doing so, we allow God to fulfill the above promise to us. And we can be sure that the "saving" He speaks of is a salvation which spreads into every nook and cranny of our being.

If we are going to give ourselves completely to Christ, then we will begin living as He lived. Christ's purpose will become our purpose. The way He spent His life should be the way we spend our life. And as we do this, the "orange cones of safety" begin appearing in the right places, protecting us from the world's evil and from ourselves.

As we give ourselves to Him, one of Christ's most effective weapons can become a part of our arsenal. It is the *Weapon of Selflessness*. Doesn't that sound like an oxymoron! How can selflessness be a weapon!

Let me explain. Jesus Christ, God's Son, gave Himself for others. As His children, we should do the same. I believe it is no accident that the One who spoke of giving us an "abundant life" also spoke of spending our lives for others.

- Sacrifice brings security.
- Meeting others' needs meets our needs.
- Doing God's deeds in God's name defeats our depression.

The *Weapon of Selflessness* is not meant to gather dust in our arsenal. God reminds us that if we attempt to hold on to this weapon, it quickly rots, becoming ineffectual. It is only in giving Selflessness away that we gain use of and benefits from it.

How does the *Weapon of Selflessness* work?

It's quite simple. We can't truly focus on more than one issue at a time. If we concentrate on looking around us for people to help, we can't be looking at our own problems. If we spend time and effort working to repair the wounds in others' lives, we won't be guilty of navel-gazing. And alleviating the fears of those in difficult circumstances means our fears are more likely to disappear because of the little attention paid to them.

Let's look at one more promise from God to *you* before we close this discussion. It is found in Proverbs 1:33 (emphasis added).

> *"But whoever (that's you!) listens to me will live in safety and be at ease, without fear of harm."*

So:

1. Give control of your life to God, listening to Him always;
2. Follow Christ's example of helping those in need;
3. Allow God's orange safety cone to protect both you and the lives of others.

Remember: Safety. Always.

# KNOWLEDGE IS POWER

Today I want to introduce **Strategy #2: Invest Your Time in Something Outside Yourself.**

The father sat on the rickety park bench watching his two daughters ride the carousel. He couldn't avoid noticing the fading paint and chipped woodwork on the merry-go-round. Nor could he ignore the rather seedy man leaning tiredly on the control lever. The wind from the ocean tossed trash all around him. How he wished he could ride on something exciting and clean and safe with his daughters! Could there be such a place? He smiled as his imagination kicked in. There wasn't anywhere on the planet like "a family park where parents and children could have fun together." So, he decided he would create it! Walt Disney stood up from his park bench and changed the world.

Perhaps the most famous quote Walt Disney is known for concerns the long-lasting nature of his theme parks. "Disneyland will never be completed. It will continue to grow as long as there is imagination left in the world. It's something that will never be finished. Something that I can keep developing and adding to."

Depression shrinks our world. Our focus; our concerns; our sense of reality all contract until we can barely focus on ourselves, much less the world around us. Our gaze turns inward, and we fail to see the world around us. Imagine your life as a set of concentric circles. As you descend into depression, your ability to focus on things in the outer circles of concern diminishes. Soon, your ability to focus moves inward, dropping out of those outer circles until all you can focus on is the innermost circle of your depression.

What if we could change our focus? What if we could enlarge our scope of reality?

The second strategy I want to discuss is this: **Invest your time and energy in something bigger than yourself.** Turn your focus outward for just a few moments onto something that is outside yourself. Mark discussed the need to reach out and help others. This is one place to start. Look at someone else and see his or her needs instead of your own. Now, this is counterintuitive to depression. But, when you focus on someone else; when you begin to think of endeavors that have an effect on someone else, you begin to move out of that center circle and move toward the outer circle.

Then, as you begin to move your attention away from yourself, you will find that your mind is able to focus better. Once you have done this, find something to do to help others.

Begin to look at other people as more than just warm bodies. They have souls. And these souls have an eternal destination. What if you could invest your time and energy in helping someone find a better relationship with their family, friends, or even, God? What a legacy you will leave behind!

There are also scientific studies showing the benefit of this type of thinking. [13]

**"Studies have shown that the act of giving can activate**

the area of the brain associated with positive feelings, lifting your spirits, and making you feel better the more you give."

When we focus on endeavors that will outlast our lifetime on this planet, we realize we are leaving a legacy very powerful and very meaningful. Mark and I are continually amazed at how this book helps our readers. We receive emails almost weekly saying how this book has "saved my life." When I feel my depression returning, I think about how God has used my illness to help others suffering from depression. I moved out of my tiny circle of misery and stepped out into a larger circle when I decided to co-author this book. I took a chance and allowed my depression to be used to help others. Mark and I will never know this side of heaven how many lives God has changed through our depression. But, it is a comfort. When I find myself afraid to look at the man in the mirror, I remember the stranger who has benefited from my pain and can face life bravely and without fear.

My form of this strategy is known as **O.A.K.** or "Ordained Acts of Kindness." Most of our readers have heard of "random acts of kindness." But, when we are depressed, our ability to see beyond the shadowy shroud of our depression prevents us from seeing such "random" opportunities to look outward. I have discovered in my walk with Christ that there are many divine appointments God has placed in my path. These encounters are NOT random. God places such events in our life to keep us from always looking within. Particularly in depression, we can fail to see the needs of others around us. In my own depression, I fail to recognize when such an opportunity is nearby.

**What we must do, particularly in depression, is to make ourselves look through that obstructive cloud of**

sorrow and self-pity and pierce the veil with empathy for others.

We must train ourselves to look for opportunities to show acts of kindness as these are not truly random. They are "ordained."

How can you do this?

There is an acronym for instituting Ordained Acts of Kindness or O.A.K. Where does the mighty oak come from? A small, innocuous acorn. A.C.O.R.N. Here it is, simply put:

*A is for Action.* We must actively look for opportunities to invest in the lives of those around us. We cannot passively wait for the chance to show kindness to others.

*C is for Christ-like.* Jesus Christ's greatest commandment was to love one another. Show love in your actions. At times, we may not feel much love for ourselves. But, Christ showed his love for us in that while we were yet sinners, he died for us and showed us the greatest love of all time. Be a mirror to the light and love of Christ and not a curtain enclosing your depression. Purposely reflect the love of Christ into the lives of others!

*O is for Ongoing.* Acting in kindness is NOT a one-time event. It must become an ongoing, daily process, and we must transform the way we think about the people we encounter. Think back to those habits. Make it a daily habit, an Ongoing habit to look for opportunities to show Ordained Acts of Kindness.

*R is for Relationship.* In reaching out of our dark depression, we create micro-relationships; moments of light in the shadowy darkness around us. Our moment of helping someone may be the only light they will see in their own darkness. And, in those moments, we create relationships that may one day prove to be long-lasting.

*N is for New.* We must look for "uncomfortable" situations, situations that challenge us to step out of our carefully constructed "boxes" to help others. The more "out there" these encounters, the farther from our depression we move.

So, go "nuts" for Jesus. Be an "A.C.O.RN." for Ordained Acts of Kindess, O.A.K., and see if it doesn't pull you out of your self-isolation and depression. After all, there was one person who made the ultimate sacrifice to help men and women who would never see or hear His spoken words. Christ is our ultimate example. For, instead of focusing on His coming death, He placed a towel around his waist and washed his disciples' dirty feet — a simple act of service that still resonates today.

Your *Weapon of Knowledge* for Today is Strategy #2: **Invest your life; invest your time; invest your energy in something or someone that transcends your life, and the rewards will be eternal!**

## LIFEFILTER #20

Today, I will:

- Follow Christ's example of helping those in need by turning my focus outward to give a helping hand to others.

- Thank God for reaching out to me through Jesus Christ.

Scripture To Strengthen Me:

"Then he said to them all: 'Whoever wants to be my disciple must deny themselves and take up their cross daily and follow me.'" Luke 9:23

**21**

**DAY TWENTY ONE**

# THE POWER TO CONQUER

Sue hummed to herself as she laid the dress out on the bed. A single parent, widowed for two years, it had been hard going to keep the bills paid and her ten-year-old daughter properly clothed. With a lot of work and a little luck, however, she had done it. Tonight was going to be a small reward for all the long hours. A bonus from her job had allowed her to buy the dress. An invitation to a party with some of her friends beckoned from the dresser. Sue hummed and smiled as she anticipated the evening.

"Mom, can I talk to you a minute?"

Sue turned to see her daughter briefly stick her head in the bedroom and then head to the kitchen. She followed. "What's up, Katie?"

"You know Sandra, don't you?" Katie asked. "She wants to know if the two of us can hang out at the mall for awhile tonight. That would be great, wouldn't it?"

Sue tried to be careful how she framed her answer. "Katie, you know I don't mind you spending time with Sandra. But I've already told you that going to the mall at your age without some supervision makes me uneasy. I trust you, but I don't trust some of the people you might encounter there." She picked up a memo pad. "Tell you what, give me Sandra's phone number, and I'll talk to her mother. Maybe one of us will be able to take the two of you to the mall later this week."

She was not prepared for Katie's reaction.

"I hate you!" the ten-year-old screamed. "You don't trust me, and you never let me have any fun. All the other mothers let their girls go to the mall. Why can't you?"

And with that, Katie ran from the kitchen.

Sue shook her head and tried to calm down. She picked up her daughter's dirty dishes from the table, rinsed them off and put them in the dishwasher. When Katie calmed down, she'd talk to her daughter and tried to discover why the girl had reacted so strongly. There had to be more beneath the surface than she was sharing.

Katie, running down the hall, was seething. Her mom didn't want her to have any fun! She cared only for herself! Didn't she see how she was hurting Katie?

Passing her mom's bedroom, she saw the dress lying on the bed. Here was a way to hurt her! Before she could really think about it, Katie picked up some scissors and began making huge cuts down the length of the dress. "There," she thought, "that should teach her a lesson!" Then she went to her own bedroom and waited for the punishment that would surely follow.

Fifteen minutes later, Katie realized her mother wasn't coming. She tiptoed down the hall until she could peek around the corner of the doorway. There was her mother, stretched out on the bed, face down, sobbing into the ruined new dress.

Instantly, Katie realized the horror of what she had done. Anger gave way to shame. Indignation fled in the face of embarrassment. Instead of the warm bond, she usually felt with her mother, a cold wind seemed to push them ever farther apart. Going over to her mother, Katie put her arms around her and said, "Mom, I'm so sorry. Take me back. Please take me back."

Have you ever blown it with God? Totally, radically blown it?

I have. And it made me feel cold and alone. Even after I'd asked God to forgive me, I still felt alone and unclean. After all, I reasoned, my sin was deliberate and enormous. I deserved to suffer. And, thinking like that, suffer is exactly what I did. The abundant life promised by Christ now seemed impossibly far away. My prayer life dwindled to nothing. Why should God listen to a miserable person like me?

Then I remembered the story of the Prodigal Son. Talk about someone blowing it! He took his inheritance (earned by his father, not him) and left against his father's will. He refused to take any responsibility for the farm, leaving more work for everyone else. And then he spent in a few weeks what it had taken his father a lifetime to accumulate.

From there, the Prodigal Son's life took an immediate plunge. Penniless and alone, he was reduced eventually to living, working and eating in a pig pen -- and the pigs were eating better than he was! Finally (his head must have been as hard as mine) he came to his senses. Cheeks blushing with shame, the wayward young man turned his steps toward home. Maybe his father would let him work and eat with the slaves. He knew it was all he could expect and more than he deserved.

As he turned the last curve that would bring him in sight of the house, a whirlwind hit him. The son found himself totally embraced by love. Let's let God's Word tell the rest of the story:

> *"But while he was still a long way off, his father saw him and was filled with compassion for him; he ran to his son, threw his arms around him and kissed him. The son said to him,*

*'Father, I have sinned against heaven and against you. I am no longer worthy to be called your son.' But the father said to his servants, 'Quick! Bring the best robe and put it on him. Put a ring on his finger and sandals on his feet. Bring the fattened calf and kill it. Let's have a feast and celebrate. For this son of mine was dead and is alive again; he was lost and is found.'" (Luke 15:20-24)*

The son, if you didn't realize it, is me . . . and you.

He didn't deserve forgiveness, but his father gave it to him. That's called *grace*.

He was absolutely bowled over by the love of a father who was watching every minute for his son to return. That's the *love of God*.

And upon his return, he was given more than he could have ever expected. That's called *restoration*.

Earlier in this book, I told you that one of the most valuable lessons I've learned is to:

**Trust in God's Word, not my emotions, as my final authority.**

When the two don't agree, it's my emotions that need changing, not the Bible. And when I finally quit letting emotions dictate my spiritual temperature, I became able to accept God's undeserved forgiveness. The abundant life He promised gradually became a part of my daily experience.

God took me back.

Are you like me? Have you done something that haunts you in those quiet moments when you're alone? If so, the story of the Prodigal Son -- which is the story of God's forgiveness and love -- is for you. All He wants is for you to return and acknowledge your wrong-doings.

If you decide to do this, be sure to look up quickly. You'll discover a Heavenly Father rushing to embrace you in His love and forgiveness. In fact, He's waiting for you right now.

And don't worry. He *will* take you back.

# KNOWLEDGE IS POWER

I sing solos. I act in dramas. I speak easily in front of hundreds with no fear or nervousness. In my heart, I am a natural-born ham.

Why then was I cringing in fear in my bedroom with the door locked? Why did my heart race with terror whenever the phone would ring? Why did I peek out the front windows of my foyer before racing across the den to the kitchen in fear someone would be at my front door? Why would I wander aimlessly around a shopping mall for hours avoiding going home for fear someone outside my family would be waiting for me?

I was depressed. It was the worst episode I had ever experienced in my forty years of life on this planet. All it took was one well-deserved remark and my entire world -- no, my entire universe -- crumbled around me. All the carefully constructed excuses, works, obligations, and dreams fell apart like wet paper.

There is no need for me to go into the details. Suffice it to say my life collapsed, and nothing was left. I awoke the next morning with a heavy, loathsome beast crouched on my chest.

His name was Fear. I avoided personal contact with any of my friends, including my pastor, Mark Sutton. In a letter, I resigned from all my obligations at church. I refused to talk to anyone. I withdrew into a comfortable, safe, dark cocoon of depression.

How could such a dramatic change come over me, Mr. Outgoing Personality, Mr. Take- the-Center-Stage, Mr. Confident Leader? Depression is that powerful. It is the David that slays the Goliath; the mouse that frightens the elephant; the spark that ignites a consuming fire.

I tell you this because I have been there. If you are depressed, I KNOW how you feel. I've had the unreasonable fear, the sleeplessness, the loss of energy, the sheer feeling of wanting to do absolutely nothing but just fade into my surroundings. Let me repeat. I know how you feel!

Why do bad things happen to good people? Because bad things happen to God's people. It is His way of growing us, refining us as iron sharpens iron. It is God's way of putting us through the crucible of suffering so we can be there for someone else who is in need. Someone else who may not have access to the Savior we have. At the time, this doesn't make the suffering any easier. And, when you're in the midst of it all, you can't see God's Big Picture. You're merely trying to survive. In today's devotion, I want to share one tool with you that helped me defeat depression and remain a tool for keeping the beast at bay.

The foundation of the doctor-patient relationship is the H&P. Those letters stand for History and Physical. The first thing a doctor does when he meets a patient is to communicate with him/her and obtain the History of the patient's illness. The doctor asks questions that allow him to systematically cover all of the possible symptoms of any disease. Then, the doctor performs a Review of Systems, asking questions pertinent to each organ of the body. Finally, the doctor touches the patient, prodding, poking, listening as he completes the Physical Examination.

Early on in my counseling, I obtained a journal. On one side of the page was a short devotion for each day of the year, (in my case excerpts from *My Utmost for His Highest*) and in the adjoining column space to write my thoughts and feelings. I would end each day by reading my Bible verse and the devotion. It was amazing how God had set up each selection to speak to me about the very events I had been going through on that day! In the empty space, I would jot down my thoughts about my day, analyzing my wayward thought patterns. Then, like the sun dawning on a new day, I would discover new insights in light of God's Word. Some days, I would be so down I could only read and merely scrawl, "God help me." Other days, the victory would be so sweet I would run out of room to write. The key was discipline, following a plan every day to do something about my depression.

Like the H&P, there were three parts to my daily entries. Reading the Bible verses was like taking a History. By looking at the world through the eyes of the Bible, God's words from the past, I could ponder my own immediate past. What mistakes had I made this day? What sins were in my life? Where had I taken my eyes off of Jesus?

The Review of Systems would become reading the devotion, an orderly progression through a system of interpreted scripture. The devotion always took me from the beginning to the end; from the general to the specific; from confusion to truth.

And, finally, the Physical Examination of my own personal soul took place as I poured out my heart onto the written page. Studies have shown that "expressive writing" may help people cope with the emotional fallout of stress, trauma, and unexpected life events that can lead to depression. These studies show that writing for ten to thirty minutes at a time, for one to five days a week; or weekly for four weeks produce dramatic improvements. Other creative outlets can also benefit and are seen in "art therapy," "music therapy," "dance therapy," and "animal-assisted therapy."

As the weeks progressed, I would be able to look back on events in my past. When I was undergoing a particularly stressful day, I could review my past and see that I had made a significant change in my life. It also reminded me that God helped me through those difficult times. I was a survivor! All this made my current problems seem smaller and more manageable. After a year, I retired the journal and started a new one. I discovered depression came to visit less and less often. And, when it did, it stayed for shorter periods of time. Whenever the unwelcome visitor arrived, I could take up my journal and revisit the suffering of my past and the victories God gave me over depression. I took my own spiritual H&P! Such an analysis always managed to put my current problems in the proper perspective.

Today, depression still lingers at the edge of my life. But it is an infrequent intrusion. And when it does hit, it bounces off quickly. Routinely, however, I dust off the old H&P of my past illness and recall a time when I was very sick. Rereading my journal is good preventive medicine. I am learning from my past and avoiding repeating my mistakes. And, I use the medicine of daily **LifeFilters**!

> Want a good suggestion for defeating depression? Your answer is today's *Weapon of Knowledge*: **Develop a daily routine.**

Take a daily spiritual H&P and such as the routine of writing it down in a journal that contains a daily devotion. It's good preventive medicine.

## LIFEFILTER #21

Today:

- I will remember that God loves me, even when I fail!

- I will believe that my Heavenly Father is always waiting with open arms to take me back.

Scripture To Strengthen Me:

*"So he got up and went to his father. But while he was still a long way off, his father saw him and was filled with compassion for him; he ran to his son, threw his arms around him and kissed him."* Luke 15:20

# SECTION FOUR

HOW CAN I CONQUER DEPRESSION FOREVER?

It looks as if Bruce and I will fight depression as long as we are on this earth. Of course, God could choose to heal us at any moment! But until that happens, He is using our depression to help thousands and thousands of other people like you and us. That's because we have discovered how to live with depression victoriously. In other words, we might deal with depression, but it no longer conquers us. Instead, through the promises of God, we are conquering depression as Christ works in us on a daily basis. We no longer fear it. We are now using our depression as a tool to glorify God and help His kingdom!

Would you like to do the same thing? You can.

As we move toward the final portion of this book, it's time for us to begin putting into place a plan that will help you move forward and daily conquer depression. We've already given you several basics, which we'll review later. However, as we start finalizing the plan, it's important for you to understand this:

**This plan must be used *every day*, no matter how you feel.**

I can't stress this too strongly: when you are depressed and don't feel like doing anything, *you implement the plan anyway.* When you're feeling good, and you don't think you need the plan . . . that is the point when you *really* need it. In other words, make this plan become a daily habit. Trust us, after awhile you work the plan almost without thinking. In other words, you *regularly defeat depression in your life.*

Okay, let's get started changing your future for the better!

## 22

**DAY TWENTY-TWO**

# THE POWER TO CONQUER

Are you ready to begin building the final phase of your plan to defeat depression for the rest of your life? Remember, God says this is not only possible; He promises it is so! 2 Peter 1:2 is particularly aimed right at you:

> "Grace and peace be yours **in abundance** through the knowledge of God and of Jesus our Lord."

Look again at those words: "**in abundance.**" If you're like many depressed individuals I've talked with, peace and grace seem in short supply in your life. But it doesn't have to be like that! The key to obtaining grace and peace in abundance is found two verses farther down in 2 Peter 1:4. It says, in part:

> "He has given us his very great and precious promises, so that through them you may participate in the divine nature, having escaped the corruption in the world caused by evil desires."

Our plan is simple but powerful and effective. We are

making you aware of God's "great and precious promises." And, we are showing you how to both believe them and then implement them daily.

I want to introduce the plan with a story from my childhood. I grew up in a national park. Hot Springs, Arkansas is surrounded by beautiful mountains, cold streams, and lush valleys. One of those valleys is what we called "The Gorge." There were picnic tables, places to camp, and inexpensive cabins you could rent. The whole valley had abundant shade and a beautiful stream running through it. A pipe jutted out from deep in the mountain, and cold, clean, mineral-rich water flowed out of it constantly. People would come from all over with empty bottles to fill at the pipe. My family went there often, and some of my happiest memories were spent at The Gorge.

If you could make it across the stream, it was possible to climb the mountain and play in the trees. But crossing the stream wasn't easy. There was only one spot where it was shallow. There, a chain of rocks led from one side to the other. Once the water had gone over the rocks, it fell into some rapids. Not dangerous, but COLD! You could use the rocks to cross without getting wet . . . IF you knew which rocks to trust. These were embedded in the river bottom and would not move. The others, however, seemed to delight in rolling and plunging you into a frigid bath.

I had carefully worked out which rocks to trust. Sometimes a friend would come with me to The Gorge, and I would run across the rocks, telling my friend to follow. Invariably, he would step on the wrong rocks and go into the water. I would laugh and laugh. Then the day came when one of my friends caught me and threw me into the water, as well. I discovered it wasn't very funny when you were the one wet and cold, so I stopped.

**Think of "goals" as stepping stones in the water. They keep you from drowning and allow you to move forward and make progress.**

Each stone not only helps you get across a difficult stream, but it also shows where you've been. If the stones are too far apart, you'll miss the next jump and fall into the water. If you quit putting down the stones, you'll be stranded in the middle of the stream, unable to continue.

Are there goals in your life? Do you know what they are?

I'm amazed at the number of people who come into my office for counseling who seem, to the casual observer, to be successful people. A careful look beneath the surface, however, often reveals they are floundering. As I ask them what they want from life, they may be able to articulate several goals: happiness, wealth, a good marriage. But when I ask them what they are doing to ensure reaching those goals, they usually give me a blank stare. They know the goals they've set seem unattainable, but they don't know why. The problem is often this: their goals, while worthwhile, are too far from where they are presently. The stones are too far apart.

It's important to know where the stones are in your life.

**For example, did you know you're putting down stones at this moment? Whether you realize it or not, the process of reading this book each day causes you to set – and reach – small goals.**

Look back through this book. Twenty-one firm stones form a path which leads you away from hopeless depression and toward a healthy emotional life. That's twenty-one goals you've set and reached. Each goal is not only a stepping stone, it also becomes a part of the firepower in your weapons' arsenal, making you even more powerful and accurate.

What other goals can you set and try to reach? Before you begin trying to set some, remember not to place them too far from where you are – unless you can put down smaller, closer goals that allow you to reach your ultimate destination. For example, you might set this goal: "I want to conquer my depression." That's a great goal! If you could get there, you'd have a weapon that would blast depression to smithereens. But how do you get there? That's where some smaller daily and weekly goals become necessary. Let's look at some possibilities:

1. I will continue to learn more about what causes depression;
2. I will read one chapter in this book each day and try to apply it to my life;
3. I will find a physician with whom I am comfortable and allow him/her to help me with my depression;
4. I will pray to God every day, regardless of my emotional state.
5. I will trust God's Word, not my present emotions, as my final authority.
6. I will always carry a **LifeFilter** with me, looking at it many times a day.

You could add many more to these six. These are only to get you started. Let the list be as long as you wish. The important thing is for these goals to be attainable and to lead you in the right direction.

Take a moment to honestly reflect on your life. What ultimate goals would you like to set? Now, what smaller goals do you need to place in front of you to build a path which will lead you to that ultimate goal?

Be careful. You must avoid falling into the trap of saying something like this: "I've tried some of this before, and it has never worked. Why should it work now?" This kind of reasoning is always wrong! That's because it presupposes you can never change. Just because you failed in the past doesn't mean you'll fail now. After all, you've grown wiser and more knowledgeable over the past several years. You also have more tools, like this book and a growing faith in God, to help you succeed.

**And remember:** *As a Christian, your future will always be brighter than your past.*

In the New Testament, Paul gives us an excellent example of how to set and meet goals regardless of what has happened in the past:

> *"I want to know Christ—yes, to know the power of his resurrection and participation in his sufferings, becoming like him in his death, and so, somehow, attaining to the resurrection from the dead." (Philippians 3:10-11)*

In these two verses, Paul sets his ultimate goals. Then he admits he hasn't reached all of them yet:

> *"Not that I have already obtained all this, or have already arrived at my goal." (Philippians 3:12)*

But is this great man discouraged because he hasn't yet completed all these worthy goals? Not at all! Instead, he tells the reader he intends to keep on putting down stones – keep on adding weapons to his arsenal – as he moves forward in his life:

> *"But one thing I do: Forgetting what is behind and straining toward what is ahead, I press on toward the goal to win the prize for which God has called me heavenward in Christ Jesus." (Philippians 3:13-14)*

Did Paul ever fail? Certainly. Sometimes he failed quite spectacularly. Did this stop him? No! Look again at the above words. Paul uses strong images like "strain" and "press." The apostle is making a deliberate effort to move in a forward direction towards Christ and away from a hurtful past.

Paul was a powerful Christian. You can be like him. Use the *Weapon of Setting Goals* to accurately focus on overcoming depression and moving forward toward a healthy, joyous life.

Place your stones carefully. Set your goals wisely. And press on.

# KNOWLEDGE IS POWER

Good morning and welcome to the Stressbuster Clinic. I am Dr. A. Drenalin, and I am here to help you. We are specialists in the SEAS syndrome. What is that, you ask?

The SEAS syndrome is the fastest-growing malady in today's culture and has nothing to do with ocean travel. Most of the population of the modern world is afflicted with this disease. Don't worry. It is not a contagious condition like the flu.

What are the symptoms?

**First,** you feel overwhelmed by information and technology. It seems that the world is coming at you so quickly you barely have time to catch your next breath before you are flooded with the next barrage of information. There was a time when you could multitask and keep it everything straight. But, lately, you've been having problems with concentration. You can't seem to remember things as quickly as you once did. You lose your keys, your wallet, your glasses. But, you never are without your smartphone or your tablet! Heavens no!

**Second,** you live under a cloud of formless, nebulous

uneasiness. You have the constant feeling that at any moment, something bad is going to happen. You are paranoid. Someone is going to steal your identity. A co-worker is gunning for your job. The cashier is going to make a copy of your credit card! You even begin to suspect that the very people you love and care about are talking behind your back! In fact, you find yourself worrying about the smallest, most insignificant things!

**Third,** you have this mixed feeling about sleep. You have so much to do you don't want to waste time sleeping. You have to win that next level on your video game. You have to meet your friends for a late happy hour. You must watch that movie you downloaded. Or, you may simply have lots and lots of work to complete. At the same time, you crave the comforting embrace of a warm bed, soft covers, and a dark room where you can close your eyes and just rest for a few hours. And, there are times when you slide under the sheets, turn out the light, and stare at the darkness for hours waiting for the sleep to come.

**Fourth,** you are just bone tired! No energy. You can't put one foot in front of the other, especially in the morning when you ooze out of bed and stare at the thing in the mirror! You fantasize about your first cup of coffee. You hoard the energy drinks. You cannot make it through the day without these things to prop up your failing energy. You are exhausted!

These symptoms are but a few of those suffered by those afflicted with **SEAS**. What is SEAS?

- Stress
- Exhaustion
- Anxiety,
- Sleeping problems

And SEAS leads inexorably to depression. Burned out, stressed out, worried out, dead dog tired, falling asleep at work or lying awake all night you have SEAS!

What can you do? The answer is found in the acronym, REST!

*RELAX*

Relaxation is the way to offset Stress. There are many ways to relax. Listen to soothing music. Go for a walk. Take a long, hot bath or soak in a spa. Get a massage. Go on a hike. Visit the beach. But, DON'T veg out in front of the TV. That can be far from relaxing!

There are other more formal methods of relaxation, such as breathing exercises and massage therapy. The bottom line is to find the best way for YOU to relax and then to use that method whenever stress hits!

*EAT WELL and EXERCISE*

Did you know that researchers in Great Britain looked at depression and diet in more than 3,000 people over five years? The following foods were more likely to be associated with depression: processed meat, sweet desserts, fried food, refined cereals, and high-fat dairy products. Katherine Zeratsky, R.D., L.D. of the Mayo Clinic had this to say about this relationship between depression and diet: "anything that comes in a package, refined or processed foods, alcohol, or anything that contains sugar, sweeteners, food additives or preservatives should be minimized, if not avoided entirely." [14]

What can you do about your diet that will help depression? People who eat a diet rich in fruits, vegetables, and fish are less likely to report being depressed. Some studies have shown that omega three fatty acids, the fat found in fish, helps prevent depression.[15]

So get out of the line at the fast-food joint and stick with fresh fruit, fresh vegetables, and fish! Limit those other food types and stay as far away from processed food as possible. We'll talk more about exercise in days to come.

## SLEEP

We are robbing our brains of critical downtime when we do not get eight hours of sleep each day. And, studies have shown you NEVER make up for lost sleep! Rest-deprived brains experience memory loss and hallucinations. Without regular sleep, brains fail at more basic tasks, and new experiences fail to become long-term memories unless brains have downtime for review.

Have you heard of REM sleep? Rapid Eye Movement sleep is that deep sleep when your brain kicks into reorganization mode. It takes a while to reach this level of sleep. REM sleep is absolutely essential for your brain to have the opportunity to reorganize, shuffle those thoughts, play out unresolved conflicts through dreams, just to name a few. Recent studies have shown that when a person goes for long periods of time without going into REM sleep, catastrophic results can occur. Have you read about video game players who go days without sleep and have sudden death? No REM sleep!

Don't worry. Missing a couple of nights of deep sleep will not endanger your life. But, the very fact that losing sleep can be potentially deadly should remind us all that each and every night, we need a good eight hours of sleep. It is NOT wasted time!

## TURN OFF THE TECH!

As I mentioned earlier, turn off the tech. We can barely get through three waking hours without working. New research shows that the average smartphone user checks their device 150 times per day, or about once every six minutes! Data from government surveys from 2011 shows 35 percent of us work on weekends on the average of five hours of labor, often without compensation -- or even a thank you. The other 65 percent were too busy to answer surveyors' questions! So, take a Tech

Sabbath, a long weekend without technology. Focus on one thing at a time!

Your *Weapon of Knowledge* today is: You may have **SEAS,** and if you do, you will need **REST**! If you are suffering from Stress, Exhaustion, Anxiety, and Sleeping Problems, then it is time to take a R.E.S.T, Relax, Eat well and Exercise, Sleep, and Turn off the Tech. When you do, you will have listened to the instructive words of Dr. A. Drenalin, and you will be able to fend off depression!

# LIFEFILTER #22

Today, I will:

- Make a list of goals I can work toward that will help me conquer depression.

- Take a R.E.S.T. from the things that cause stress.

- I will praise God for helping me move toward a wonderful future.

Scripture To Strengthen Me:

"Brothers and sisters, I know that I have not yet reached that goal, but there is one thing I always do. Forgetting the past and straining toward what is ahead, I keep trying to reach the goal and get the prize for which God called me through Christ to the life above." Philippians 3:13–14 (NCV)

# 23

# DAY TWENTY-THREE

# THE POWER TO CONQUER

It's time to turn the tables on depression! Today, we're going to give you a powerful addition to your arsenal of depression-defeating weapons. This particular one is a vital part of the top three of all the weapons you're assembling and learning how to use. Let's review the other two:

1. Above anything else, you *must* have an ongoing relationship with Jesus Christ.
2. You must make the decision that you will believe – and act upon – the promises in God's word, *not your emotions*.

This third weapon actually depresses depression! Before I reveal what it is, let me tell you about a lesson I learned as a boy. At some point in my boyhood, I got a boxing clown for a birthday present. This inflatable toy had a round bottom and was painted to look like a clown. The idea was to hit it as often as you wanted. Maybe it was supposed to help you learn how to box; if so, I was a miserable failure. In any case, this opponent was a pushover – literally. It never tried to fight back, never defended itself, never got mad at me. Always smiling and standing still, it presented a beautiful target I could pummel to my heart's content. But a funny thing happened with the boxing clown.

I lost every fight I had with it.

I was the one doing the punching and the knocking down. I was the one who should have won. But the clown had a secret. Because of its round bottom, it never stayed knocked over. No matter how many times I punched the clown's lights out, it always came back upright. By the end of the fight, I was exhausted. Punched out and worn out, I was ready to quit. But my opponent, the clown, still stood there, smiling that infuriating grin at me. When I left the room, I sometimes imagined it raising its arms in victory behind my back – smiling all the while, of course.

**Perseverance is the name of our new weapon.**

Coupled with faith in Jesus and a reliance on His promises, it allows us to conquer any depression that comes our way! One of the first things it does is help us break a deadly cycle we may not even be aware of. And breaking that cycle produces some positive side-effects: new, powerful habits that actually act as our allies.

How does the *Weapon of Perseverance* accomplish all this? First of all, let's take a look at this deadly cycle. When we notice depression's arrival, what is our reaction? In my counseling and discussions with depressed people, I've discovered we initially react in one of two ways. Some of us are always caught by surprise. We never expect the depression to return again, and can't see it coming until it has completely surrounded us. Others of us know our depression is pretty regular; we understand its signs and can watch as it approaches and settles in.

That is the first stage of the cycle of depression. But

whether we are surprised by its appearance, or whether we see it coming, we often react in the same way to the cycle's second stage . . . and this is the part that is most important . . . and deadly.

Let me talk directly to you for a moment. After realizing you are experiencing a depressive episode, how do you react? If you are like many I've counseled, you give up. You throw up your hands and say, "Depression is here again. There's nothing I can do about it." And then you let the disease dictate how you will react emotionally. Black moods and periods of doubt control you until the depression leaves and the cycle, for the moment, is complete. Then you wait, without realizing it, for the next cycle to begin.

But what if you changed the cycle? Believe it or not, it is within your power to do so.

**Again, you may not be able to stop depression from descending on you, but *you can choose how you will respond to it*.**

I don't know how many times I've already stated this in these pages, but I want to pound this into your thinking.

Here's where the *Weapon of Perseverance* delivers a mortal blow to your enemy. Quite simply, you "tell" depression: "I'm never giving *up* or giving *in* to you. You might continue to plague me, but I'll fight you with everything I've got. My emotions don't belong to you, and I refuse to let them be held hostage without a fight. You might knock me down, but I've decided to keep on getting up. And I'll fight you every time."

What does this type of attitude accomplish?

- First of all, it breaks your usual cycle. You no longer simply give up when depression hits you.
- Second, the process of deciding to fight depression,

*even when you don't feel like doing so*, begins to give you more control over your emotions and helps you no longer feel like a victim.
- Third, as you decide to fight depression every time it appears, you build confidence in yourself. In many cases, this shortens the amount of time depression stays with you.
- Fourth, using the *Weapon of Perseverance* on a regular basis builds powerful habits in your behavior. Use it long enough, and eventually you begin fighting depression when it appears without even realizing it!

Let me give you a word of encouragement. Even a little effort on your part each time is helpful. Even if you can't successfully fight off depression this time, but begin trying to do so, *you have made progress.* Making the decision to do what you can each time will make you stronger.

Perseverance pays off.

Flash back to 1968. The Mexico City Olympics are taking place amid great fanfare. As the marathon contestants line up, spectators buzz about possible winners of the race that gave birth to the entire Olympic movement. Most of the attention focuses upon Mamo Wolde of Ethiopia, and rightly so; he will be the eventual winner of the marathon.

But he will not be the only winner that day.

With the crack of the starter's gun, the contestants begin their quest for a gold medal. One of the runners, John Stephen Akhwari of Tanzania, finds himself trapped in the middle of some other runners several miles into the race. Unable to see well, he falls and hurts his leg horribly. He watches in anguish as the other racers continue on. The marathon will not be won by John Stephen Akhwari on this day. He has come to Mexico City and failed . . . or has he?

Now flash forward to the end of the race. Wolde, the Ethiopian, has already won. An hour has passed, darkness is falling, and the last spectators are leaving the stadium. Suddenly their attention is drawn to the sounds of police sirens. The marathon gate to the stadium is thrown open and, unbelievably, a lone runner stumbles into the stadium for his last lap. It is John Stephen Akhwari. Hobbling painfully on his bandaged leg, grimacing with every step, knowing he cannot win the race, he continues all the same. Finally, he crosses the finish line and collapses.

Why, someone asked him, didn't he stop after injuring himself? After all, there was no way he could win the race. Listen to John Stephen Akhwari's response. "My country did not send me to Mexico City to start the race," he said with dignity. "They sent me to finish the race." [16]

Perseverance is a powerful weapon.

Let's flash back 2,000 years to another man who knew how to persevere. The apostle Paul was a man who devoted himself wholly, unselfishly, to God. But it certainly did not ensure him a life of pleasure and ease. You could say his life was maxed out with beatings, persecutions and, to add insult to injury, multiple imprisonments. These prisons, I might add, had no weight rooms, color television, or time off for good behavior. In addition, some of Paul's peers criticized the Apostle for getting himself into what they believed were embarrassing circumstances.

Paul, put in prison once more, could have given up. Instead, he had this to say:

> *"I am not ashamed, because I know whom I have believed, and am convinced that he is able to guard what I have entrusted to him for that day." (2 Timothy 1:12)*

Paul knew God would not fail him. He believed that the

Christian who stayed faithful, even in the tough times, would be ultimately blessed for his/her perseverance.

God has a special place in His heart for those who endure. Man's power doesn't interest Him. Dynamic personalities and great people skills don't impress Him. He sees through smiles and designer clothes, looking for something more.

> "The eyes of the LORD are on those who fear him, on those whose hope is in his unfailing love." (Psalm 33:18)

**If you're giving the best of yourself to God and trusting in Christ to save you, then the Heavenly Father's eyes are on *you*.**

He blesses you every time you get knocked down by depression and then get up, still trusting God and still willing to live for Him. You see, looked at in this way, depression does not make you a failure. Instead, it makes you a strong Christian and a winner in God's eyes.

So even if depression keeps knocking you down, make the decision today to keep getting up. Let Paul's creed also be yours:

> "Therefore put on the full armor of God, so that when the day of evil comes, you may be able to stand your ground, and after you have done everything, to stand." (Ephesians 6:13)

Keep on standing.

# KNOWLEDGE IS POWER

I was cleaning out my study and came across a tiny spiral notebook. An orange cover showed the image of a seagull flying against a sunset. The first page inside carried one word: "Pax," the Latin word for peace. The next page carried these words:

> FUTILITY
> In starry silence I sit, wondering
> Where life has flown!
> With all of eternity beaming on me
> Stars gleaming and yet dead for millennia
> My moment of life, pitiful existence, is fleeting –
> Smoke in the wind of time – Ashes that swirl in
>     a gale
> And yet!
> I dare to strive; to dent; to mark this universe
>     with my existence!
> Striving against adversity –
> However futile –
> Is the essence of Humanity!

I recalled the night I wrote those words. After an exhausting day on the wards during my internship, I walked up the last stretch of stairs to the roof of the hospital. I sat in the freezing cold night air and looked at the stars above me. Why was I here? What was the meaning of life?

I was depressed at my situation. I had chosen the wrong field of medicine, and I was miserable as I watched my patients dying all around me in spite of every effort to save them. I was depressed, but this was long before I recognized the symptoms of depression in my life. My solution was to write something down. I have always been a storyteller, a writer. I had always dreamed of being a published author. Writing, for me, saved me from my depression. This little notebook I carried in my white coat pocket became my antidepressant! The words scrawled in that little notebook saved my life.

**Strategy #3 is: Find a Creative Outlet.**

When we are depressed, our minds are far from creative. Depression is a deconstruction of our souls, our minds, and our emotions. Eventually, depression can deconstruct our bodies. The antithesis of deconstruction is construction. Building up. Creating!

When our minds turn to creativity, we are using a different part of our brain than the part that is steeped in depression. This will not be easy. But, the mere act of thinking creatively sparks the process of rebuilding those damaged synapses; replacing that low neurotransmitter.

Wait a minute, you protest! I am NOT creative in the least! I can't sing a note! I can't draw a line! I can't write a poem! Well, my friend, this is simply a lie! We are made in the image of God, and God is the Creator of the Universe. Alice Bass, in her book, *The Creative Life,* says: "The foundation for our creativity is our Creator. Because we are made in the image of God, our creativity and our faith are intertwined."[17]

Did you read that carefully? We are MADE to be creative! And, our creativity is a reflection of our faith! How do we ignite that spark of creativity? There are four aspects of creativity that EVERY person has.

**Imagination.**

Imagination is more than just an exercise in playful storytelling or role-playing. Imagination is how we visualize every single problem and challenges that face us and then develop a way to overcome those obstacles. Bass says, "Imagination is part of our nature: we solve problems, we relate to others, we come up with ideas, we make guesses, we are resourceful, we dream and fantasize."

When we use our imagination, we are bringing to bear all of our experiences, personality, abilities, and intuition. Imagine that! So, go ahead. Imagine. Dream. Open your mind to endless possibilities, and the spark of creativity will glow and grow into a flame.

**Explore and Experience**

I have shared with our readers my experience in defending the realm of the Christian faith, a discipline known as apologetics. When I began to fulfill Romans 1 by exploring God's creation, I was shocked, amazed, dismayed, and in awe of God's incredible creative power. Our universe with billions of stars and galaxies is a tapestry of God's cosmic palette. The images from our space telescopes alone are stunning revelations of the fingerprint of God! So, here is my challenge to you. Explore God's world. Experience God's power. Open your closed and depressed mind to the majesty that is all around us. What you will find is that this universe in all of its grandeur and design was made for us to enjoy. This is how much God loves us!

**Use Your Tools**

God has given each one of us a spiritual gift. You have one, probably many. These spiritual gifts can be a tool for exploring your creativity. And, whether or not you admit it, God has given you a unique talent. It may not be music or art or the written word or dance. You may be an excellent seamstress. You might be a fantastic organizer. Think of that. You create order from chaos! Isn't that what God did with the universe? My point is we each have gifts, talents, and skills that God is just itching to use. When we use these tools, we begin to taste just a hint of the wonderful creativity that is from our God!

**Worship**

Finally, realize that when we are creative, we are in worship. Bass says: "To enjoy a creative life we need to be free to experience more of Christ's inspiration and less of our own inhibitions, fears, and sin patterns. We live a creative life in response to the Lord Jesus as he is revealed in the Scriptures and by the Holy Spirit. . . . Your relationship with God gives you insight into his purposes and his creative process. Your creativity is a link to the living God."

Remember: Psalms 139:13-14 tells us,

*"For you created my inmost being; you knit me together in my mother's womb. I praise you because I am fearfully and wonderfully made; your works are **wonderful**. I know that full well." (emphasis added)*

**Today's *Weapon of Knowledge* is this:** Creativity is the best way to move out of your suffocating depression into God's wider world.

You can find a creative outlet and you should. Don't think for a moment that you are not creative. "Every day, you have the opportunity to offer something of yourself, your ideas, your perspective, the work of your hands. And every day you are taking in the offerings of others. Creativity is a big part of your life."

# LIFEFILTERS #23

Today, I will:

- Rest in the fact that God will never give up on me.

- Resolve to fight my depression and not give up!

- Remember that I am created in the image of God, "fearfully and wonderfully made" (Psalm 139:14).

Scripture To Strengthen Me:

*"Therefore put on the full armor of God, so that when the day of evil comes, you may be able to stand your ground, and after you have done everything, to stand." Ephesians 6:13*

# 24

## DAY TWENTY FOUR

## THE POWER TO CONQUER

Let's talk about vampires for a moment.

No, I don't believe in them; I don't even like books or movies about the blood-sucking monsters. My imagination is already vivid enough! But focusing on vampires will provide us with a good example of another weapon we can add to our arsenal that just might stop depression in its tracks.

According to the various stories about these creatures, vampires are super-strong; they can move at lightning speed. Let them get close to you, and they can supposedly overwhelm your emotions and make you fall under their spell. Even worse, normal weapons cannot hurt vampires. Try to beat them using only your own strength, and you'll lose every time.

Do those characteristics remind you of anything? Super-strong, attacking before you know it, able to take over your emotions, impossible to beat in your own strength: come to think of it, that sounds a lot like depression! But – and this is important – vampires have one major problem: they cannot stand the sunlight. Expose these monsters to the light of day, and they disintegrate into dust.

When you are in the middle of a severe depressive episode,

if you're like most of us, all you want to do is stay inside, alone, curled up in the dark. Depression thrives in such an atmosphere. It gains power as it slinks through the darkness of your situation. It laughs at your feeble attempts to stop the negative, sluggish emotions that encircle you. The farther it can push you into solitude, the darker will be your thoughts and memories.

**But don't forget: depression is a liar.**

It only seems to be unbeatable. It fears the moment you begin moving into the light. As you expose your depression to the light of God's word, as you decide to believe the promises of scripture instead of your emotions, depression trembles. And when you learn how to use this next weapon, you form a powerful combination that kicks depression in the teeth!

Jesus is the Light of the world. You already know that. But the Bible clearly says that Jesus created the universe and everything in it. That means that the Light of the world also made the light of *this* world. Think of your emotions as a plant. The more sunlight you receive, the better your spirits will grow, and the more beautiful your life will bloom. Read what scientists are now saying about the sun and your depression: "A sunny day may do more than just boost your mood -- it may increase levels of a natural antidepressant in the brain. A new study shows that the brain produces more of the mood-lifting chemical serotonin on sunny days than on darker days." [18]

Exercise and the right diet are also parts of this weapon. Combine them with your being outside in the sunshine, and you'll probably find your depressive episode weakening . . . or even going away entirely! In the next section of this chapter, Bruce will discuss why this works so well. But right now, just take my word for it. Sunshine, sweat-inducing exercise, and the right diet work wonders!

I have a confession. I'd like you to think I'm 6' 2", about 185 pounds, in whip-cord shape with almost no extra body fat. In reality, I'm shorter than 6', and if I ever reach 185 pounds, my family will think I've become anorexic. The moment I was born, the doctor took one look at me and said, "Put that baby on a diet!" Since that moment, I've been on some kind of diet nearly all my life. A snail could outrace my metabolism. If I don't eat right *all the time*, I'll gain weight immediately.

In other words, I'm not one of those guys who loves to live at the gym and pump iron. In fact, I have to grit my teeth to make myself work out. And even after I'm done, I still resemble the Pillsbury ® Dough Boy more than I do Arnold Schwarzenegger. But I've come to realize that my body gets a real lift from regular, sweat-producing exercise. I might be tired when I begin working out, but by the time I'm finished - and especially about an hour later – I can feel more energy coming into me. As I go through the day, my emotions are higher, my attention better, and my ability to make decisions stronger.

In short, exercise works!

I'm not saying you have to lift weights or spend hours doing aerobic exercises. But anything: long walks, jogging, basketball, swimming, or any other sport can help raise your heart rate, your energy level, and your mood.

Your body is important; don't neglect it. The Bible says:

> *"Do you not know that your bodies are temples of the Holy Spirit, who is in you, whom you have received from God? You are not your own; you were bought at a price. Therefore honor God with your bodies." (1 Corinthians 6:19-20)*

"Honor God with your body." Certainly, this means living a morally pure life. But you can also use those words as the impetus to begin a regular program of exercise. In doing so, you give Jesus Christ, and yourself, a better "temple" in which to live.

Let me leave you with two rules that act as a reminder of what you've learned today:

**Outdoor Rule #1:** Give each day to God. As the sun shines down on you, you'll also find God's Son shining down on you. The sun dissipates the shadows of night. The Son destroys the shadows of depression.

**Outdoor Rule #2:** The higher you raise your heart rate in exercise (within the prescribed limits recommended by health professionals), the higher you raise your spirits.

It's time for you to leave the indoors and discover God's world. Your depression will try to stop you. It will help you think of all kinds of excuses to keep from weakening it. But remember, you've already learned that together, you and God are stronger than your depression. So say no to your emotions and get out into the sunlight!

## KNOWLEDGE IS POWER

The mountains soared above me, arching their green, rocky spines towards a perfect blue sky. I moved with the grace of an Olympic runner, my legs slicing through the cool air, my lungs filling with life-giving oxygen. A perfect moment in time and space, my mind at peace from a "runner's high." San Diego stretched away beneath me as I ran along a road on the mountain ridge. In the far distance, the ocean sparkled with foam. I could not imagine being anywhere more wonderful.

I never saw the rock.

Perhaps a small boy had thrown it at a snake along the path; or perhaps a tremor in the bedrock of the earth had dislodged it from the perch where it had resided for millennia, awaiting my arrival. The forces of nature conspired against me to place the rock perfectly under my foot.

I fell across the running path, pain lancing up my left leg. Nausea clouded my vision, and the pain was unbearable. As my eyes cleared and the perfect clarity of the moment faded with the growing pain, I glared at the rock, a tiny stone that had felled me. Later, I learned I had stepped on the rock and twisted my ankle so severely, I would have to maneuver around

San Diego in a wheelchair. My running days were temporarily at an end.

At this time in my life, I had been jogging three miles a day for almost a year. In the weeks after the injury, as I returned from my vacation, other people noticed a change in my personality. I became agitated and angry from the least provocations. I seldom smiled and would reply to inquiries with the demeanor of a mad pit bull. I was not totally unaware of the changes in me. I noticed I had trouble sleeping, difficulty concentrating. In short, by giving up on my daily exercise, I had become angry, agitated, and depressed. It was as if I were withdrawing from a powerful drug.

In fact, I was. The "drug" was exercise.

The most dreaded word in the English language must be the "E" word. I am not speaking of exorcism, although most people would rather be exorcized than exercised!

Why do we dread the idea of exercise? Most likely it is because we have become a sedentary nation, plopped down on our couches in front of the cable television or glued to the internet. At the University of California at Berkeley, School of Public Health, an ongoing survey clearly showed:

> **A strong association exists between a sedentary lifestyle and depression. However, studies have shown that exercise is necessary, in fact, almost mandatory, in the battle to defeat depression.**

Why did I become depressed when I could no longer exercise? Why is exercise so essential to overcoming depression? You may recall an earlier discussion of the "economy of movement" that comes with depression. Remember how the body slows down as the synaptic pathways from the brain fail to function properly? Scientists have discovered a substance called *endorphin*. Endorphin affects the brain, similar to the effect achieved when a person takes a narcotic such as morphine. In fact, narcotics work on the endorphin-stimulated areas of the brain.

Endorphin is released by the nerves working with the exercising muscle to limit the pain associated with exertion. Studies have shown that the exercise of muscles also increases the levels of serotonin in the brain and can have an effect that may last for two weeks! The combined effects of elevated serotonin and the euphoric effects of endorphin give you a relaxed, stress-free feeling. If exercise is so important, how can you avoid the negative stigma associated with the "E" word?

Newer studies have shown that regular exercise can generate new neurons! Improved blood flow to the brain (and to those hungry, hungry hippos) signals your genes to produce more growth factors which spur nerve cell growth.

If exercise is so important, how can you avoid the negative stigma associated with the "E" word? The main concept is movement. Movement and physical activity will produce the same changes in your brain chemistry. Thirty-five minutes of walking fast five times a week or, sixty minutes a day three times a week significantly improve symptoms of depression. Studies have shown that exercise was about as effective as cognitive-behavioral therapy or antidepressant medications in reducing symptoms. This suggests that if you suffer mild to moderate depression, you may avoid drugs by using exercise as an acceptable substitute.

If you are loathe to exercise, then try walking up and down the stairs instead of using the elevator. Park at the far end of the parking lot and walk a longer distance to your work or to the store. Look for every available opportunity to *MOVE*. You will be surprised how the time can add up and bring about the desired improvement. Of course, always consult your physician before starting any exercise program.

A word to the wise: be patient.

Studies have shown it takes at least a month of sustained exercise to notice a significant mood-elevating effect. Also, remember this isn't a competition. Your exercise program should be enjoyable. Take it nice and easy and don't increase the strenuousness or duration of your workout more than 10 percent a month. Exercise shouldn't be a chore. It should be fun!

An interesting study regarding the motivation for exercise points out a significant difference in the way we approach our *movement*. Contrary to popular belief, this study demonstrated that people who exercise regularly year in and year out are not motivated by the desire to control weight or improve their physical appearance. They do not respond to *negative* goals. Rather, they have a desire to seek the reward of consistently feeling relaxed, focused, and alert. These people stick with their exercise because exercise brings on a sense of pleasure and contentment. This study showed that regular *moving* released tension, counteracted depressed feelings, and combatted food cravings. Make the decision to take up some form of movement, and you will feel better after the first effort.

You don't have the time? Wrong!

We never *have* the time to exercise. The point of this study is that desire is the important ingredient. If you are motivated to exercise out of a sense of obligation, then you will never *have* the time. Something else will always be more important. But, if you desire to exercise, then you will MAKE time.

No time? Make time! Your *Weapon of Knowledge* today is simple: Move!

## LIFEFILTER #24

Today:

- Weather permitting, I will get outside and enjoy the sunshine God made for me.

- I resolve to begin (or continue) a regular program of exercise.

- I will stop and thank God for sending His Son, Jesus Christ, to forgive my sins and live with me forever.

Scripture To Strengthen Me:

"Do you not know that your bodies are temples of the Holy Spirit, who is in you, whom you have received from God? You are not your own; you were bought at a price. Therefore honor God with your bodies." 1 Corinthians 6:19–20

# 25

# DAY TWENTY-FIVE

# THE POWER TO CONQUER

It began with a cough. Only appearing in the winter, it seemed but a minor inconvenience. I preached with a cough drop in my mouth, and that took care of it. Several years went by. By now, I was used to the winter cough — no big deal.

Then, about four years ago, winter finished its season, but my cough decided to stay. Now, it racked my body, kept me up at night, and began affecting my energy. To make it worse, my wife, who never complains and is the most positive person I know, went through a series of health problems, needing several surgeries and requiring some long recuperation periods. Trying to help her while having little strength myself made things even more frustrating.

I now found myself coughing until I gagged or threw up nearly every afternoon and evening. I had little energy and could barely stand up without feeling like I was going to faint (which I actually did – twice – at the hospital; it's a good way to get their attention!). After several diagnoses, I underwent three different surgeries. It certainly helped some, but I was still weak and battled the persistent cough. One day it dawned on me that getting back to normal might never happen.

A severe time of depression hit me. It was the deepest, darkest time of my life. I had felt so bad for so long that I asked God to let me die. Obviously, He didn't answer my prayer. Instead, He led me back to the Bible – His message for me (and you). As I read God's promises to His children, and as I once again read about Paul's plea to be healed (not answered),

**The Lord whispered in my heart, "I want to use your weakness as a witness to others. My grace is sufficient. Soak yourself in the scriptures and lean completely on Me."**

Since that day, Mayo Clinic diagnosed me with pulmonary fibrosis, a disease that is incurable and always fatal. The usual causes are smoking or being around asbestos a lot. I've never done either. The University of Florida Medical Center performed a lung transplant on me, and now I'm doing much better. I still have problems, but I've learned to pace myself. I'm determined to keep going. My goal is to stay positive as I remember the memorized scriptures that are promises from my Heavenly Father.

Chronic pain; constant fatigue; unrelenting difficulty. Some of you reading this book not only fight depression, but you also have one or more of these unwelcome companions. If so, this chapter is especially for you. I know how you feel. You are fighting enemies on several different fronts, and are hampered by both physical and emotional fatigue.

If this describes you, then please read carefully these next words:

*Through all your pain, fatigue, and depression, you CAN still live a victorious life!*

For people like us, there are several steps we **must** take in order to achieve victory and overcome depression and its allies.

- Use one of our **LifeFilters** every day. Carry it with you and read it at least ten times during the day (constant reinforcement). The next day, carry a different one with you and do the same thing. When you get to the end of the 30 **LifeFilters**, start over.
- Work this program – every chapter (day). Don't skip anything.
- Don't confuse your physical state with your spiritual state. Even in pain, weakened by disease, you are still loved by God and surrounded by His care.
- Focus on the scriptures below; believe them; memorize them; apply them.
- Don't ask, "Why, God?" Job never learned why. He simply remained faithful and, as a result, that faithfulness during incredible suffering has blessed millions of believers. Instead, ask, "God, what do You want me to learn from this? And, use this for Your glory."
- You don't have to hide your pain or pretend it's not there. Instead, point out to others how God is sustaining you in the midst of your difficulties. By doing this, you control the pain, fatigue, and depression, using them for God, not giving in to them.
- As you talk to others, don't magnify the pain in your life. Instead, magnify God's power to sustain you.

Here are your "lifeline scriptures" – all from Psalms:

*"The LORD is my rock, my fortress, and my savior; my God is my rock, in whom I find protection. He is my shield, the*

*power that saves me, and my place of safety." (Psalm 18:2NLT)*

*"You are my hiding place; you will protect me from trouble and surround me with songs of deliverance." (Psalm 32:7)*

*"The* Lord *is a refuge for the oppressed, a stronghold in times of trouble. Those who know your name trust in you, for you,* Lord*, have never forsaken those who seek you." (Psalm 9:9–10)*

*"The righteous cry out, and the* Lord *hears them; he delivers them from all their troubles. The* Lord *is close to the brokenhearted and saves those who are crushed in spirit." (Psalm 34:17–18)*

What did you notice about the above scriptures? All of them talk about focusing upon the nearness of God to *you*. So, focus much upon God, especially in the tough times. Ask Him – and believe He will answer your prayer – to keep you faithful until the end.

One more thing before we close. Here's your homework! Read every one of these scriptures until you both understand them and you have integrated them into your life. Memorize all of them and go over them regularly. This may mean that you spend several days in this chapter. That's okay! Your goal is not to finish this book quickly. Instead, it's designed to help you change how you think and act. When you know these scriptures and are using them during life's tough times, then move on to the next "Day."

Remember: in Christ, fatigue cannot stop you; pain cannot define your life; depression will no longer control you. After all, God is your source of strength!

# KNOWLEDGE IS POWER

I came home one day to find my wife in her recliner with two heating pads, one on her knee and the other on her wrist. I thought she had fallen playing tennis. But, instead, she had swollen, painful joints over her entire body. She was in so much pain, she couldn't walk. She couldn't grip a glass to drink water. The symptoms had come on rather suddenly, and I literally watched one of her fingers swell right before my eyes! I was very alarmed and made her a doctor's appointment immediately.

The doctor made the diagnosis of stress-induced fibromyalgia. As we learned earlier, the diagnosis of fibromyalgia was laughed at by "serious" physicians. But, recent studies have revealed there is a physiological condition underlying the pain and swelling of muscles and adjacent joints.

Cytokines. No, this is not some science fiction monster from Doctor Who or Star Trek. Cytokines are "immunomodulating" molecules. They modulate or control the immune response of the body. Christina Van Pymbroeck, Ph. D. had this to say about the relationship between stress, depression, and cytokines:

> "When a stressor occurs in sufficient strength whether it is a psychosocial or physiological threat, the organism mounts a vigorous defense through the immune system, leading to high levels of circulating cytokines which can evoke both depressive symptoms and pain as part of the array of sickness behaviors designed to protect and defend the individual. In this view, the frequent co-morbidity of depression and pain arises because each symptom is a manifestation of the same homeostatic drive to conserve energy for survival."[19]

Don't worry. I will help you understand what you just read, for it is one of the most important comments about pain and depression you will ever read. Let's unpack that very dense set of sentences and see if we can make sense.

When a person undergoes stress, the body mounts an **immune response.** This immune response is just like the kind of activity the body undergoes to fight off an infection such as the flu. The mediators of this response are chemicals known as cytokines.

The **cytokines,** in inducing this immune response, produce what is called sickness behavior: behavioral changes such as restlessness, reduced activity, sleepiness, and social withdrawal; changes in thinking such as lack of concentration and loss of interest; and mood changes such as depression. Think back to the last time you were sick with a bad cold or the flu. This is exactly how you felt, wasn't it? Now you know why.

The purpose of this kind of **"sickness behavior"** response is to slow the person down, to reduce movement and activity in order to conserve energy. In other words, it is a **protective response.** In my wife's case, she was overstressed by having to take care of her sick, homebound mother, and also caring for our daughter. The stress of trying to balance these two demanding roles and run our household was more than she could handle. Her body was simply saying, "That's it! I'm shutting you down the only way I know how. If you are hurting and inflamed, you can't move, and this is the only way I can get you to stop long enough to heal!"

This sudden onset of **pain** and inflammation isn't the end of it. The symptoms of pain and stress and depression can feed upon one another and lead to a "chronic" malady. In other words, chronic pain and unrelenting depression tend to feed off one another. The brief "shut down" sequence becomes prolonged as the stress turns into depression and the days wear on. The pain and swelling become non-stop. Muscles and joints ache constantly, and the person develops fibromyalgia. Fibromyalgia is widespread chronic pain and a heightened and painful response to pressure on muscles, joints, and even the skin.

> Your *Weapon of Knowledge* today is: **There is an intense relationship between chronic pain, stress, and depression.**

In fact, some studies suggest that we can't tell which comes first, the stress or the depression or the pain! It is an extremely complex situation.

What can be done about it?

**First**, recognize that your symptoms are real and not just "in your head." There is a definite "physiologic" reason for the pain and inflammation.

**Second**, recognize that the fibromyalgia or chronic pain and the depression go hand in hand. You must treat BOTH to get rid of the symptoms. You cannot just treat the depression and get rid of the chronic pain. Nor can you just treat the chronic pain and get rid of the depression. In fact, the newest approved therapies for chronic pain turn out to be anti-depressants as well!

**Third,** if you suffer from chronic pain from an illness not brought on by depression, realize that with time you will suffer from depression. And, if you are suffering from chronic depression, you will in time, develop chronic pain. The two go hand in hand.

**Fourth,** you must find a physician who is willing to admit that fibromyalgia is a real disease. Fortunately, the older tier of physicians such as my generation who were taught that fibromyalgia was not a real disease is being outnumbered by newer, younger physicians who recognize this relationship between inflammation, stress, pain, and depression.

**Fifth,** get help! Don't suffer in silence. My wife went to our physician, and he gave her the truth in no uncertain terms. You have to reduce the stress in your life, or you will hurt like this from now on. There is no lasting treatment for the pain. You have to deal with the stress and the depression in your life. My wife had to make changes in the way she was taking care of her mother, and it made all the difference in the world. Her pain went away when the stress decreased.

Recognize, right now, without a shadow of a doubt, that there is a relationship between chronic pain, stress, and depression. You have to attack all three axes of this trifecta, or you will continue to suffer from pain AND depression. It will require changes in your lifestyle, your behavior, and will require you to find a physician. Once again, I remind you that you MUST partner with a physician if you are to conquer depression!

Don't suffer in pain alone! Get help!

## LIFEFILTER #25

Today, I will:

- Remember that in Christ, fatigue cannot stop me, pain cannot define my life, and depression will no longer control me.

- Devise a plan that will attack my chronic pain, stress, and depression (review Day 25).

Scripture To Strengthen Me:

"The righteous cry out, and the Lord hears them; he delivers them from all their troubles. The Lord is close to the brokenhearted and saves those who are crushed in spirit." Psalm 34:17–18

# 26

**DAY TWENTY-SIX**

# POWER TO CONQUER

What is your purpose in life? Yes, I'm talking to you! Depression can make a person feel worthless. We've already seen how its lies will pull you far from others and make you feel inadequate to do anything for the Lord. But, remember that we've decided to believe God's truths in His word, not our fickle emotions. So, look once more at the following verse:

> "For we are God's workmanship, created in Christ Jesus to do good works, which God prepared in advance for us to do." (Ephesians 2:10)

Let's personalize the above verse. After all, "us" includes you!

"For **you** are God's workmanship, created in Christ Jesus to do good works, which God prepared in advance for **you** to do."

In other words, **you** have a purpose. God has certainly put **you** here for a reason. And, interestingly enough, when **you** embrace your purpose, you'll discover another powerful weapon to fight depression is automatically added to your arsenal.

Joseph Scriven was happily and deeply in love with a young woman. He proposed marriage; she accepted. As plans matured for their wedding, Joseph's joy seemed to grow daily. Then, just days before the wedding, his fiancée drowned in a tragic accident.

Scriven fell into bitterness and a deep depression for months. At his worst point, however, he turned to Christ and found grace and peace. Shortly afterward, this young man used his own gifts to touch the others in this world who, like him, had suffered tragic losses. He penned a hymn that is still blessing people around the world: "What a friend we have in Jesus, All our sins and griefs to bear!" [20]

How did Scriven leave his depression behind? Through a combination of looking to Christ for help and looking for others to help. And if you'll only look around as you walk through life, you'll discover there are always others who can use your help. No matter how little money you have, there are others who have even less. No matter how depressed you are, there are others doing even worse. No matter how few friends you may have, there is someone who is achingly alone.

Your weapon for today is simple: get out and find others to help. Ephesians 2:10 suggests that you have good works to perform that will touch those around you. Discover their needs. And then use your own gifts and resources to help put their lives back on track. In the process of doing this, you will find your depression fading in strength. It will be replaced by a feeling of satisfaction and completeness. Why? Because in helping others, you are doing what God has placed you here on earth to do.

Could you get in the habit of doing this every day? I'm not suggesting that you'll always find someone to help. But simply by training yourself to look outside your own neediness toward the needs of others, you can begin holding depression at bay.

To explain how this works, let's take a look at a saltwater

aquarium. Did you know that one of the most popular aquarium fish is the shark? Yes, you read that last sentence right! You might wonder how a shark could possibly fit in a regular-sized aquarium. This can happen only because of the unique properties of the shark. If you catch a small shark and confine it, the shark will stay a size proportionate to the aquarium. In other words, sharks can be six inches long yet fully matured! But if you turn them loose in the ocean, they will grow to their normal length of eight feet.

**What is the size of your spiritual aquarium?**

Depression encourages you to keep to yourself. It wants you to focus only on your own needs. There within its dark, quiet environment, it is easy to engage in endless speculation of your own life and its myriad problems. If you succumb too long to depression's seductive emotions, however, you'll find yourself smaller emotionally, less developed as one of God's children, content to live out your life in the frigid, dark waters of your own small aquarium.

Could the above paragraph be talking about you? If so, it's time to break out of the cold, dark aquarium of self-absorption and discover the wonderful depths of the ocean of life. Use this weapon: *"I will focus on the needs of others every day"* to grow in God's love. In doing so, you'll discover you're not the only one in this world who needs love, patience, and a kind word. And when you give each of those to someone in need, your heart and spirit will grow deeper, higher, wider, and happier. In other words, you'll grow into the person God has always planned for you to be.

Go out and get growing!

## KNOWLEDGE IS POWER

Up to this point, we have discussed three strategies. Today, we look at Strategy #4:

**Exchange virtual relationships for real relationships.**

My wife and I made our way through customs and emerged in the airport in Auckland, New Zealand. To say I was nervous was a huge understatement. Here we were halfway around the world, leaving our adult daughter who suffers from epilepsy at home. We were to meet Sherry's good friend, Alex, and her husband, Grant for a three-week tour of New Zealand. Three weeks in a foreign world with two total strangers! I couldn't imagine a more potentially disastrous situation.

Sherry met Alex playing bridge online. Online! They had spoken via video chat, but we were about to place our lives in the hands of someone Sherry had met *online*! I recalled telling my kids never to trust anyone they met online. And yet, here we stood beneath the statue of an enormous orc from the "Lord of the Rings" movie searching the crowd for two strangers.

Before I tell you how this encounter turned out, let's look at some other examples of the influence of our current information technology on people and their virtual relationships "online."

A study published in 2006 by the Massachusetts Institute of Technology Press's journal, Presence showed that nearly 40% of men and 53% of women claimed their virtual friends were *equal to or better than their real-life friends.*

In our busy world, people are increasingly isolated and unattached, and they have no community to call their own. To fulfill the longing to fit into a group of people to whom they can relate, they turn to virtual communities.

We see this at least three forms of virtual communities:

- *Video gaming and alternate online realities*
- *Social media*
- *Pornography.*

With regard to **video gaming and online alternate reality communities**, the question is: why is the idea of virtual reality so addictive? In his book, Hooked on Games: The Lure and Cost of Video Game and Internet Addiction, the author Dr. Andrew Doan says,

> "It helps to understand the basic human needs that motivate people to seek satisfaction through a virtual source. Such needs include: satisfying curiosity, providing a sense of purpose in life, heightening a sense of invincibility, feeding the ego, offering companionship, satisfying the need for challenges, gratifying the need to be a leader, fulfilling fantasies, and meeting the need for love and acceptance."[21]

In The Demise of Guys, Phillip Zimbardo points out that when we invest our time and energy in virtual relationships, we lose the simple skills of direct interpersonal communication.

We no longer know how to look someone in the eye. We no longer know how to develop intimacy and true friendship. We become socially isolated and when confronted with real-life situations, socially awkward.

What we see in our current culture is increasingly isolated individuals who meet their basic needs online and never have to invest in real, face to face encounters. The result is a world of socially awkward people who have no idea how to create and maintain physical relationships!

In the case of **social media**, the attractions can be a sense of anonymity. We can create a persona and say and do anything we want without fear of retribution. Civil discourse and kindness and respect are no longer parameters that frame our interactions. We can curse, scream, throw a tantrum, and vilify anyone we want on the fly. How many times have you seen this play out in the media? A famous celebrity vents on Twitter or Facebook and then just minutes later retracts and apologizes online.

In real life, interaction face to face, we use the skills of discernment and respect to temper our responses. But, with more time spent in online interaction, we are losing these skills as well. Not only are we facing the loss of interpersonal communication skills, but we are also losing the ability to engage in physical intimacy.

In *The Demise of Guys*, Zimbardo has this to say about **pornography**:

> "Most young men today will tell you that they visit porn sites. Some of them will even enthusiastically describe to you the features of their favorite sites. Given a choice between online pornography and going out on a date with a real girl – that is to say, a girl who doesn't look like a porn star and isn't wearing lingerie – more and more young men tell me that they prefer online porn. 'Girls online are way better looking,'

one young man said to me, with no apology or embarrassment."²²

Zimbardo goes on to say that a recent study from the Centers for Disease Control and Prevention (CDC) found that

> "Regular porn users are more likely to report depression and poor physical health than nonusers are. The reason is that porn may start a cycle of isolation. Porn may become a substitute for healthy face-to-face interactions, social or sexual."²³

The bottom line is that we are exchanging virtual relationships for real relationships. These virtual relationships are much easier and require less "work" than interacting with real people.

The effect of this disconnect from real life is the development of anxiety, stress, and depression. I have mentioned this before, and it is worth repeating. **Depression among young adults is at an all-time high, and their immersion in the digital world is a large part of the problem.** So, what can we do about it?

Mark and I both want to encourage you to *reach out to real people.* Isolation in the digital world can become very dangerous. Where can you start? Why not at a church? Attend a worship service. Go to a church-sponsored special program or event. Find a Bible study group of people with similar interests. God never intended us to live as islands in isolation. We are part of His family, His Church, and in those settings when we are surrounded by real, genuinely caring people, we can discover a truth that Christ conveyed to His disciples on His last night with them. He said,

> "I no longer call you servants because a servant does not

know his master's business. Instead, I have called you friends, for everything that I learned from my Father I have made known to you." (John 15:15)

Jesus went on to say, "**This is my command: Love each other.**"

**We have a friend in Jesus, and He is anything but virtual!**

Back to my story! Alex and Grant appeared with a huge banner welcoming us to New Zealand. The following 20 days were filled with surprises and delights beyond our imagination. We toured the entire country, and I must admit, I have never met more friendly people than the citizens of "Middle Earth." I had the opportunity to speak at Alex's church on depression! And, Grant's father asked me to ship thirty copies of our first book to New Zealand for a Bible study group.

Sherry and I fell in love with the people of New Zealand. We met fellow Christians, and it was like meeting long lost sisters and brothers. One day, I hope we can return to that beautiful, hope-filled country! So, you see real friendships pay off! Your *Weapon of Knowledge* for today: Take those virtual relationships and make them real! It will be challenging, perhaps even disappointing. But, in real life, you will find the stress, and the anxiety and the depression will melt away when you look someone in the eye who truly cares about you and wants to help you feel better!

## LIFEFILTER #26

Today, I will:

- Thank God for meeting my needs.

- Disconnect from the digital world and embrace genuine relationships in the real world.

Scripture To Strengthen Me:

*"Carry each other's burdens, and in this way you will fulfill the law of Christ." Galatians 6:2*

# 27

## DAY TWENTY-SEVEN

# THE POWER TO CONQUER

The young woman sat across from my desk, weeping into a sodden tissue. She had just told me her problem: she knew God did not love her. "What can I do?" she asked me. "What's wrong with my life?"

How would you have answered that question? I already knew this woman was a Christian; that part had been taken care of. Would you have explored all her past sins? Would you have assumed she was in denial about some secret misdeed?

I began by asking her three questions. But to be honest, I was pretty sure I already knew her problem. First question: "Do you acknowledge that you've sinned against God in the past?" Second question: "Have you repented of those sins and asked for forgiveness based on what Jesus did for you on the cross?"

The young woman answered yes to both questions, leading to my last question: "Are you currently feeling depressed, or do you fight depression on a regular basis?" Again, the woman answered, yes. I saw her two more times. By the third week, this formerly defeated, weepy woman no longer doubted God's love for her. She now had a much more joyful countenance.

What did this young woman discover that so changed her?

She had embarked on a simple program that started transforming her spiritual and emotional life. Below, I'll share with you the weapon I gave to the young woman that enabled her to reject Satan's whispered lies and focus on God's love for her.

It starts with this question: Does God love you? Right now, in this place, can you feel His love?

One of the greatest problems depressed people face is a difficulty believing God loves them. Interestingly, they have no problem believing God loves *other* people. But somehow, they believe the promises of the Bible are not for them.

Am I describing you?

If so, it is vital that you discover, believe, and put into use this particular weapon.

Let's begin with a basic understanding: *the reason why you may believe God doesn't love you has nothing to do with God and everything to do with your depression*. There are literally hundreds of passages in the Bible where God declares His love for you. It's not necessary to be perfect to receive God's love and be in His will. All it takes is repentance and a desire to be close to Him.

Here are several personal messages from God to you. Let's begin with:

> *"For I am convinced that neither death nor life, neither angels nor demons, neither the present nor the future, nor any powers, neither height nor depth, nor anything else in all creation, will be able to separate us from the love of God that is in Christ Jesus our Lord." (Romans 8:38-39)*

That ought to cover just about any excuse you can come up with about why God might not love you!

If you're still doubtful, listen to Christ as He speaks of God's love for you:

*"The Father himself loves you because you have loved me and have believed that I came from God." (John 16:27)*

Need more convincing? Worried you might not live up to God's love? Do you feel your life doesn't measure up to deserving these promises? Then read this last love letter from your Heavenly Father (who, by the way, *never* lies and *always* keeps His word!):

*"But when the kindness and love of God, our Savior appeared, he saved us, not because of righteous things we had done, but because of his mercy." (Titus 3:4-5)*

**"Not because of righteous things we had done, but because of his mercy."** Did you see those words? That means He loves *you*!

Dan Livingston was desperate. Terribly overweight, he had tried every diet that came along. Alas, the weight was still there and getting worse. He finally made an appointment with his physician and asked for help.

The doctor had a unique idea for Dan. "I want you to eat normally for two days, then skip a day. Repeat this schedule for two weeks and then come back to see me. By that time, you should have lost five or six pounds."

Two weeks later, Dan returned to the doctor's office. His physician was shocked to discover that his patient had lost over forty pounds!

"How in the world did you do this?" he asked.

"Doc, I just followed your instructions. But to tell you the truth, I thought I was going to die before I finished the two weeks."

"Were you that hungry?"

"No!" Dan replied. "But that skipping all day nearly killed me!"

**Any day in which you skip believing God loves you is a day in which you invite depression and guilt to take over.**

So, come back to the above scriptures every day if necessary. Carry the **LifeFilter** at the end of this chapter with you every day for awhile as your constant reminder of God's love. Nothing is stronger than remembering; at every moment, you are surrounded by the awesome love of God.

Do I practice what I preach? You bet I do. When I turn my digital phone on every morning, I have programmed it to begin with this message: "Today, God loves you!" I memorize scriptures that promise God's love for me. And I regularly listen to music which speaks of God's love.

What can you do to remind yourself of this important fact? The more you discover and believe in God's unfailing love for *you*, the more difficulty depression will have pulling you into its clammy grip.

Believe it: **GOD LOVES *YOU!***

## KNOWLEDGE IS POWER

Imagine this trip to your doctor.

"Doctor, what did my MRI show?" You ask.
 The doctor smiles at you and pulls up a set of gray images on a computer screen on his desk. He studies the images and then nods.
 "Well, do you want the good news or bad news?" He asks.
 "Good news, of course." You say.
 "Your scan is completely normal." He smiles again.
 "But, what about the pain in my head?" You ask, a bit warily.
 "Well, it will get worse if I give you the bad news."
 "What is the bad news?" You ask.
 "I could say you have a brain tumor. That would make you very sad, wouldn't it?" The doctor frowns.
 "Yes, it would."
 "Then, in that case, I will tell you whatever truth you want to hear."

Now, at this point, would you just get up and walk out the door and go home and tell everyone the "good news"? Or, would you stop for a moment and consider what the doctor is saying to you. Is he telling you what you want to hear? Or, is he telling you the truth?

You see, when your life is on the line, you desire one thing: **truth**. And, in processing these thoughts, you have made a very important conclusion. You have just relied on the undeniable fact that truth, that is, **real** truth, is very inconvenient and beyond your control. After all, if wishing something made it a reality, you could wish away any possible brain tumor from those images, and more importantly, from your head. But, the "inconvenient" fact is that truth is **transcendent**; it transcends human control. Truth is based on reality, and we cannot control reality.

We are now living in a "post-truth" culture. What does this mean? Here is a dictionary definition: *"relating to or denoting circumstances in which objective facts are less influential in shaping public opinion than appeals to emotion and personal belief."* Many Christian thinkers today have concluded that the tension between a world living the "post-truth" mindset in the midst of a world that is rooted in truth produces circumstances that lead to hopelessness and despair. Here is a quote from C. S. Lewis on the matter:

> *"If you look for truth, you may find comfort in the end; if you look for comfort you will not get either comfort or truth only soft soap and wishful thinking to begin, and in the end, despair."* C. S. Lewis

**In my counseling, the most powerful question I was told to ask about my current circumstances was, "What is the lie?"**

The assumption that set me free was that I had bought into a lie about who I thought I was and what my current circumstances were. But, to appreciate a "lie" I had to understand there was truth, and not just any truth but truth with a capital T. Why is this important?

Our culture is suffering from **"truth" decay.** We are immersed in a culture of lies. How do we discern truth? I'm glad you ask. Let's take each letter of that word in this chapter and the next and see if can come to a factual understanding of truth.

**T – The first letter in T.R.U.T.H. is Transcendent.** What do I mean by that?

J. P. Moreland, the renowned Christian philosophy, makes the point that there are bedrock principles behind reality that we cannot actually see or sense, such as the rules of logic or mathematics. These "transcendent" principles underlie the very foundation of our universe, and our reality is totally beyond our control. No matter how badly we want two plus two to equal five, it will ALWAYS equal four. And, let's face it, we WANT truth to be transcendent. Otherwise, our doctors would always "lie" to us and tell us what we "WANT" to hear instead of telling us the truth about our medical condition. If we don't know the truth, we can't ask for the treatment! This may seem to be a harsh realization. But, if you'll hang with me, I will show you how this characteristic of truth is ultimately liberating. For when TRUTH is out of our control, it provides for us an anchor; a harbor in the storm. If TRUTH is truly transcendent and beyond human control, then we can rely on its constancy in the face of the changing and turbulent emotions of depression.

**R – The next letter of T.R.U.T.H. is for Reality.**

When it comes to science, medicine, engineering, physics, and all the hard sciences we rely on the constancy of their foundation in reality; a foundation built on transcendent values we cannot physically hold or sense. We want the laws of gravity to help our car stop when we throw on the brakes! We want the antibiotic to kill the bacteria that is causing our pneumonia!

Philosophers use the "Correspondence Theory" to explain that truth is based on, or, corresponds to, factual reality. It is not based on opinion or fantasy or fiction. When in doubt, examine the facts of reality, and you will always find truth. In order to conquer depression, we must move away from our carefully constructed behavior patterns often built on misperceptions of the real world around us. Embracing the realities that often confound us can help us move away from the restrictive, smothering world of depression. We are not meant to live in the darkness!

One clear concept I learned in my battle with depression was the depth of my own self-deception. Often, in the face of the reality of my "stinking" thinking and the reality of my physical component to depression, I had to rethink all of my preconceptions based on lies and falsehoods. Here is one clear truth: lies are of human origin. Always! We are lied to. We lie to others. And, we can lie to ourselves. Facing reality can clearly demarcate the lies of our culture and the lies of our depression!

In the next chapter, we will finish the letters of TRUTH. For now, embrace the liberating idea that truth is beyond our control and is based on reality. It is a bedrock, unmovable foundation on which we can base our thoughts and our emotions. For, as you will see, Truth is more than a concept. It is a Person!

## LIFEFILTER #27

Today, I will:

- Remember that God loves me. Right now, I will stop and thank God for loving me.

- Believe that I can become the unique person God created me to be.

Scripture To Strengthen Me:

*"But when the kindness and love of God our Savior appeared, he saved us, not because of righteous things we had done, but because of his mercy." Titus 3:4–5a*

# 28

## DAY TWENTY-EIGHT

# THE POWER TO CONQUER

By now, maybe you're buying into the concept that God can actually use your depression for His glory. If so, you've made tremendous strides since the beginning of this book, and I want to congratulate you!

God's Word clearly teaches that all things which happen to us can be used ultimately for our good:

> "We know that all things work together for good for those who love God, who are called according to his purpose." (Romans 8:28, NRSV)

**The last time I checked, depression is a part of "all things."**

How can your depression be used for something good? There are several ways. Let's begin with your worship of God. Ever-expanding television channels and the rise of the internet have allowed all of us multiple choices for watching church services from the comfort of our homes, on our laptops anywhere, or listening through podcasts as we drive. This is both good and bad.

For the home-bound or others who are honestly prevented from being able to go to church, these choices are fantastic. But for those of us who are depressed, those same choices can actually become a temptation. We rationalize by saying, "I don't feel like being with others today. I'll just stay home and watch the worship service on my monitor. After all, I'm still worshipping God."

Follow me carefully here. Yes, it's good that at least you're worshipping God, even if you're at home. However . . . if you can attend church, but you choose to use your depression as an excuse to stay home, you're missing out on God's best for you. God did not create the church so that you could remain isolated. He knows you need to be among the body of Christ, surrounded by other believers.

"I'm worse than anyone else there. I want to be alone. God couldn't possibly love me." Those thoughts may be screaming at you as the time for church approaches. But you know, because you've read this book and have begun internalizing God's promises for you in His word, that those screaming thoughts are *lies from Satan*. And also remember what we learned yesterday: there are people at church who actually need your help. There are some who are struggling with depressions and no self-worth.

Imagine yourself at church this next Sunday. All around you are people with their own problems and trials. But you mainly see them as smiling and confident, because all you see is the outer façade. In your heart of hearts, it may seem as if they are worthy of God's love; you may believe He wants to receive their worship. But when you look at yourself, an unworthy, guilty person stares back. *How could God love someone like this?* You ask yourself.

It is at this point, however, that a small miracle occurs.

Those around you won't see it. The pastor and choir will never be aware of it. But as you decide to ignore your negative emotions and believe God loves you, and as you lift your heart and soul in praise of His name, I imagine angels in heaven nudging one another to stop and pay attention. All heaven begins to rejoice as, in spite of your depression and poor self-attitude, you worship God. "Worthy is the Lamb!" the celestial inhabitants sing as they join you in honoring the One who can inspire love in the face of depression.

Your fellow members never see it, but God does. He knows the sacrifice you have made to come to church, sit with others in a public place, and worship. In doing so, you have said, "God is more important than my depression. I will praise Him regardless of how I feel."

Do you remember the poor widow who put two mites in the temple treasury? Jesus watched this woman standing in line, waiting as the rich threw in a hundred – maybe a thousand – times more than she could ever afford. When it came to her turn, she gave what she could to God. Still, it was a pitiful amount. Scholars tell us Jesus, in describing this woman, chose the Greek word that meant the poorest of the poor.

And yet . . . and yet . . . Jesus said this woman gave more than anyone else!

Learn a lesson from the lips of Christ. The people saw the amount. God saw the *love* and the *sacrifice*.

**Could it be that when you worship God in spite of your depression, you, of all the other people in the church on that day, are actually the one giving the most? God sees your *love*. And He sees your *sacrifice*.**

Remember this when you go to church next Sunday. Even better, remember it every day!

## KNOWLEDGE IS POWER

William Provine was a scientist and an atheist. He made several uncomfortable conclusions about what our culture would look like when we completely embrace atheism. **First,** he claimed that there is no God. **Second,** once God is out of the picture, then there is no objective morality. Right and wrong are completely relative and in our hands. **Third,** there is no meaning to life. We are left to our own devices in finding our own meaning and purpose in life. And, **fourth,** there is no afterlife. Our death signals the end of us. His final summary of this situation states there is "**no hope**" for us as humans. No hope! Is it any wonder that in a culture that is becoming dominated by this atheistic worldview we now have the highest suicide rate in the history of western culture?

As I mentioned in the last chapter, we can combat this growing disease of depression and hopelessness in our culture by embracing TRUTH. To find our path out of the darkness of our depression, we must cling to the transcendent and reality foundation of truth. Let us continue with the remaining letters of the word TRUTH.

**U – The next letter of T.R.U.T.H. is for Universal Standard.**

In our relativist, "postmodern" culture, which began in the mid-1960's, there are some very basic assumptions. There is no *metanarrative,* which means there is no big picture to reality, no God, no purpose, no story unfolding around us. Therefore, there is no *ultimate authority* such as God, so all authority is in question and does not necessarily have to be obeyed. That means there is no *absolute truth*; no absolute right or wrong; no absolute anything. All is relative. Words have no intrinsic meaning, and we can trust no one!

Do you see what this does for us as human beings? It frees us from any restraint; any standards; any moral law. We can believe anything we want to believe at any time. What's true for me right now is true. If I want to take your wallet, I can rationalize I am entitled to that because there is no such thing as right and wrong. Hitler and Mother Theresa were both GOOD people!

C. S. Lewis makes a very interesting claim about this conundrum. When we look at a squiggly line, we KNOW it is crooked. But how? By what standard do we draw this conclusion? He said,

> *"My argument against God was that the universe seemed so cruel and unjust. But how had I got this idea of just and unjust? A man does not call a line crooked unless he has some idea of a straight line. What was I comparing this universe with when I called it unjust?"*

**Now we can see how our adversary, Satan, confounds, and confuses us by making our emotions the rule of law when it comes to morality!**

Let's face it. Our emotions change from day to day; from hour to hour; from minute to minute. If our sense of right and wrong were based on our emotions, then right and wrong would be as squiggly and elusive to pin down at C. S. Lewis' crooked line!

TRUTH being transcendent and based on reality and therefore, the basis for an objective sense of right and wrong gives us an even firmer foundation for understanding and defeating our depression. We can no longer be slaves to our ever-changing and capricious emotions!

**T – The next letter of T.R.U.T.H. is for Testable.**

The disciple Thomas is well known for his doubts. But, there is merit in being a "doubting Thomas." When we consider the account of Thomas' encounter with the risen Christ, we are comforted by the fact that Jesus did not chastise Thomas for doubting. Rather, he praised Thomas for not basing his faith on blind trust.

Here is a very important rule for us to buy into. There are many notions and gimmicks and "cures" for our emotional well being. There are many worldviews, religions, philosophies that promise a "cure" for depression. They all claim to bring us peace and contentment.

These alternative views of life promise unending happiness. Such a state is not sustainable. Why? Because, happiness is fleeting!

**What we desire as humans is joy, a continual state of contentment with our condition in life that can only be fulfilled through a relationship with Jesus Christ.**

I floundered around for years, denying I had depression and seeking all kinds of "easy" fixes for my emotional turmoil. When I finally descended into my deep, dark major depressive event, I took the test! I examined my emotions and my thoughts, and I was honest enough to admit the truth – I suffered from depression.

I finally listened to my wife. As I mentioned earlier, I had been trying to treat myself. She told me the truth. Get help!

**Don't be led astray by easy promises and quick fixes.**

Overcoming my depression was work! Hard work! I didn't get there overnight, and the cure wasn't going to happen with the snap of a finger. This book outlines a thirty-day plan, a "boot camp" that provides you with weapons and strategies to conquer depression.

Always be vigilant. Always question your emotional and spiritual state. Have a plan. And relax. Jesus gave Thomas one of the greatest complements known to mankind in response to Thomas' questioning:

> *Then he said to Thomas, "Put your finger here; see my hands. Reach out your hand and put it into my side. Stop doubting and believe."*
>
> *Thomas said to him, "My Lord and my God!"*
>
> *Then Jesus told him, "Because you have seen me, you have believed; blessed are those who have not seen and yet have believed."*
>
> *John 20:27-29 (NIV)*

Test everything! Question every quick, knee jerk treatment. Don't settle for a false cure for depression. I can tell you from my own personal experience I can only find a lasting peace when I place my faith in the one person who IS truth, Jesus Christ. Test everything as Christ instructed us in the scriptures. Be a "questioning" Thomas! For, Truth will pass ALL tests!

**H – The last letter of T.R.U.T.H. is for Human Value.**

Have you been paying attention to the media lately? Have you watched the popular shows and movies recently? There is a theme that runs through most of today's "stories." The gist of the message grows out of Provine's conclusions.

We are just glorified, highly evolved animals. There is nothing special about human beings. We "dance" to our DNA. We serve only to pass on our "selfish" genes to the next generation. Humans are NOT exceptional. Humans are just things. How does being a "thing" make you feel?

Want to know how much you are worth? I've been writing about TRUTH and the H in truth is Human Value. The objective standard of truth guarantees human beings are more than just *things*. You see, things can be bought and sold. Things can be thrown away. Things can be marched to the ovens in Auschwitz or drowned in the killing fields of Cambodia or lined up and shot against the walls in Stalin's Russia. Things can be purged and ripped from a mother's womb because she no longer desires the "thing" that is growing within her. Things can be ignored on the streets of our cities.

Culture tells us a big lie that we are highly evolved animals; we are **things** that dance to our DNA. There is nothing special in us.

Let me make one thing very clear. In Genesis, God speaks very highly of you and me when He created us.

> *Then God said, "Let us make man in our image, after our likeness. And let them have dominion over the fish of the sea and over the birds of the heavens and over the livestock and over all the earth and over every creeping thing that creeps on the earth."*
> > *So God created man in his own image,*
> > *in the image of God he created him;*
> > *male and female he created them.*
> > *And God blessed them.*
> > *Genesis 1:26-28a(ESV)*

You are made in the image of God. That doesn't mean you ARE God. No, it means you are more valuable than any material possession in the universe because you are an image-bearer of the King of King, the Lord of Lords, the Creator of all reality. And, let me transition your thoughts to an even deeper and more profound idea. You see, only one Person was also Transcendent; one divine Person Really existed; one Person took us from under a universal standard to living under Grace; one Person told us to Test everything. Finally, take that Human Value represented by the letter H and let's transform it into a radical idea. A very radical concept that changed all of human history.

**For you see, God did not count it loss to become flesh:**

*In the beginning was the Word, and the Word was with God, and the Word was God. He was in the beginning with God. All things were made through him, and without him was not any thing made that was made. In him was life, and the life was the light of men. The light shines in the darkness, and the darkness has not overcome it.*
    *John 1:1-5 ESV*

Jesus Christ, God in man form, lived through anything and everything you and I could possibly imagine. He faced childhood, pain, suffering, betrayal, hunger, stress so terrible he sweat blood, and complete and utter desertion from every friend he had. Even God turned his back on His own Son. I'd call that pretty depressing, wouldn't you?

Do you feel like God has abandoned you? Try being His only son. Why did God abandon His only son? So that Jesus Christ, part of the Godhead, a member of our Triune God would bridge the gap between our material life here on earth and our future presence with God for all of eternity. Things here on earth are temporary. They are fleeting. They will pass into the crucible of time and find themselves wanting. And, I am here to assure you beyond a shadow of a doubt that your depression can be just as fleeting and defeatable.

**The love of God as shown to you and me through the final H of TRUTH,** *His Sacrifice* **places a value on your life that is greater than all of the earthly possessions known to all of mankind.**

You and I are loved. God made us an entire universe, so we could look up at the night sky and instead of feeling small and insignificant bask in the love God has shown us in one of the most powerful love letters: His creation!

> *The heavens declare the glory of God;*
> *the skies proclaim the work of his hands.*
> *Day after day they pour forth speech;*
> *night after night they reveal knowledge.*
> *They have no speech, they use no words;*
> *no sound is heard from them.*
> *Yet their voice goes out into all the earth,*
> *their words to the ends of the world. Psalms 19:1-4 (NIV)*

In a culture that constantly lives and thrives on lies, we can find our way out of the darkness of depression by embracing TRUTH. Not just empirical truth, but personal, eternal TRUTH. Want to know truth? Know Jesus Christ.

> *Jesus said to them, "If God were your Father, you would love me, for I have come here from God. I have not come on my own; God sent me. [43] Why is my language not clear to you? Because you are unable to hear what I say. [44] You belong to your father, the devil, and you want to carry out your*

> *father's desires. He was a murderer from the beginning, not holding to the truth, for there is no truth in him. When he lies, he speaks his native language, for he is a liar and the father of lies.*
> John 8:42-44

How do we resist the lies of Satan? How do we answer the question, "What is the lie?" Simple:

> *Jesus said, "If you hold to my teaching, you are really my disciples. Then you will know the truth, and the truth will set you free."*
> John 8:31b-32

In Christ, the truth will set you free!

## LIFEFILTER #28

Today, I will:

- Go to church this weekend and worship God in Spirit and in Truth.

- Ask God to help me use this depression for His glory today.

- Never give up on life, because God's love *never* gives up on me!

Scripture To Strengthen Me:

"We know that all things work together for good for those who love God, who are called according to his purpose." Romans 8:28 (NRSV)

# 29

# DAY TWENTY-NINE

## THE POWER TO CONQUER

It's time to thank God for your depression.

*What are you talking about, Mark? I'd rather hug a porcupine. Do you know what this disease has done to me? Can you understand the emotional pain and suffering I've endured because of it? And now you want me to thank God for it?"*

I don't want you to do this... God does.

Do you remember Paul? The first missionary of the New Testament Church and the most prolific of all the New Testaments writers, this man had to learn to embrace his weakness. He tells us this:

> "To keep me from becoming conceited because of these surpassingly great revelations, there was given me a thorn in my flesh, a messenger of Satan, to torment me. Three times I pleaded with the Lord to take it away from me. But he said to me, 'My grace is sufficient for you, for my power is made perfect in weakness.' Therefore I will boast all the more gladly about my weaknesses, so that Christ's power may rest on me." (2 Corinthians 12:7-9)

We really don't know what Paul's "thorn in the flesh" consisted of. Some have theorized it was a disease of the eyes. Others believe he had a speech impediment. In any case, grab hold of this thought and let it take root in your heart: **it was God's will that this "messenger from Satan" be a part of Paul's daily life!**

Why would God do this? There are two reasons:

1. First, it was a "blessing in disguise" for Paul. He had to learn both to live with this problem and to continue loving God at the same time. Doing this taught Paul, it was absolutely necessary for him to lean completely on his Heavenly Father for daily support. His native intelligence couldn't overcome this "thorn in the flesh." A powerful personality and incredible capacity for work helped him not at all in this area of his life. Only an utter dependence upon God could make a difference.
2. Second, God received praise from others as they realized how Paul could be a powerful witness for Christ and still have these problems.

The bottom line was that *this problem took everyone's attention off of Paul and put it on God, where it belonged.*

Wouldn't it be interesting if Paul's "thorn in the flesh" had been depression! I believe that Paul, as an artist and scholar, could have easily suffered from this problem. In any case, perhaps God has allowed you and me to fight the same battle as the apostle for the same reasons: God wants us to learn more of Him and to rely completely upon Him. And God wants us to be witnesses of His power to others who suffer from a number of different problems.

Now can you begin to thank God for your depression? Because of it, you learn more about living in faith, you discover more about God's love, and you have a unique ministry to those who are hurting!

Another question: knowing the power of Christians who live triumphant lives through giving their weaknesses to God, could Satan try to keep those same believers apart from the world? Could Satan tempt us to want to be isolated, knowing that if we began to live for Christ by letting Him use our depression, we would become some of God's most effective witnesses? If this is true – and I believe it is – then it should challenge us to rise up against the emotions of depression and get out into the world. There, we can be a positive example to others who need help.

"My power is made perfect in weakness." Those words allow you and me to see depression in a different light.

**We don't have to like our depression -- Paul didn't want his "thorn in the flesh." But if we can ever get to the point where we quit giving up and feeling sorry for ourselves, we place our lives on an entirely different path.**

And if we can give our depression to God and ask Him to use it for His glory, something wonderful happens, both to others and to ourselves.

Ask yourself this question:

*Why has God chosen to let me suffer from depression? Believe me, it's not to make you feel guilty, but to help you do good.*

She was timid, scared, and suicidal. As the young woman sat in my office, she admitted to a childhood filled with abuse. Abuse that had scarred her memories and wounded her soul. Abuse that had left her depressed and consumed with guilt.

Now she wanted to die.

Several days before she had been driving in her car, contemplating how to end it all. As she turned on the radio, Jane just "happened" to hear one of my 60-second radio spots. In that one minute, God reached out and touched her heart. The flicker of hope began to build in her, and on Sunday, we found her in our church hanging on every word of the sermon.

Now, in my office, she had retreated into a shell and talked again of suicide.

Person after person had tried to help her. Because of the memories of abuse, however, she was unable to let them get emotionally close to her. To make things worse, here I was, a male, sitting across from her in a small office. I could almost see the fear beating at her, telling her to get out of the office before something bad happened – like when she was a child.

"Jane, I know a little of what you're going through because I also suffer from depression," I said.

"You!" She didn't believe me. "You get up and speak in front of thousands of people. You smile and help people all around you. How can you possibly know what it's like to be depressed?"

I began telling her about the sometimes daily battles I have with depression. I shared how insecure and guilty it tried to make me feel. When I told her of how there were days I didn't want to get out of bed, much less see people, she nodded her head. But it was as I admitted that I had to work very hard sometimes to believe God loved me as much as He loved others that I finally began to see her relax.

"How can you preach and counsel if you fight depression?" she wanted to know. I told her about some of the ways I've learned to trust in God in spite of my emotions. I explained how I've decided to believe God's Word more than I trust my emotions. And I told her of the wonderful times I've had with the Lord, even deep in depression, when I've continued to pray and read my Bible.

"Could I learn to do that?" she asked hopefully.

Not only could she learn, today, this young woman is a living testimony to the power of God in overcoming years of abuse and depression. She is using her weaknesses to help others who have not yet discovered God loves them and wants, through Jesus Christ, to give them a wonderful life.

Could I have ever reached this woman without having fought depression? I don't think so. By admitting my depression and sharing both the problems I've had and the victories I've won, God was able to use my weakness for His glory. To put it another way: a life was saved because I fight depression!

How can God use your depression? Who is waiting in the wings, lonely and confused, for a sensitive word from you? Believe me, people who need your help are all around. And as you show how you can identify through their depression, God begins both to perfect you and strengthen them.

# KNOWLEDGE IS POWER

As we draw to a close, let's stop and review some of the most important *Weapons of Knowledge* you now have at your disposal.

Remember, **knowledge is power.** The more you can learn about depression, the more you are equipped to conquer depression and find hope again. Don't just stop with this book. Open up your mind and life to other sources of information on depression. Start with your physician and your counselor. Just be careful of your sources. Remember that not all knowledge is truly reliable!

Remember the **body and mind are intricately intertwined.** The brain and body have a unique connection. Therefore, you need to understand how these components of you work together. Also recall that you will need to address all three "legs" of depression: body, mind, and soul or another way to put it your intellectual life, your physical life, and your spiritual life.

Remember that depression can be viewed as a form of **stress.** And stress can lead to growth. Growth is painful, but if you allow depression to push you forward into a healthier lifestyle, then depression can be viewed in a positive way. If you don't change and allow depression to defeat you, then true failure can occur. Press on and view your depression as a gift! Transform the way in which you think about your depression. Use it. Don't let it use you!

Remember that you must **build a team.** You need a spiritual adviser of some type, hopefully in a church-like setting to help with spiritual issues. You need a counselor or behavioral specialist to help you with emotional issues. Finally, and most importantly, you need a physician to address your physical and medical condition. All three of these components are absolutely necessary to succeed in your daily conquest over depression.

Remember, you will need a **physician.** We have discussed many factors that impact your depression from underlying illness to chronic pain to how anti-depressants work. Having a primary care physician is an absolute requirement in your battle against depression.

Remember **habits, both good and bad,** contribute to your overall condition. Identify those habits in your life and retrain your mind to respond to those emotional cues with more positive and constructive responses.

Remember, you are very likely suffering from **SEAS**: Stress, Exhaustion, Anxiety, and Sleeping Problems. The solution is Relax, Eat well and Exercise, Sleep, and Turn off the Tech or **REST**.

Remember **women and men are affected differently by depression.** Understand how depression relates to your specific gender.

Remember the four **Strategies:**

1. Turn off the Tech and take a digital-free vacation.
2. Invest your life and time in something that will outlast your life – serve in some capacity.
3. Find a creative outlet.

4. Replace your virtual relationships with real, live, breathing community.

Remember to ask yourself often, "**What is the lie?**" Remember who is the father of lies.

**Remember that truth is absolute, and the TRUTH will set you free.**

Remember that **chronic pain and depression are interrelated**. Don't suffer in silence. Attack both sides of this equation.

Finally, using **LifeFilters** and what you have learned in this book, **devise a plan** that will be robust, active, and unique to you and your situation. Stay on the plan daily, and you will find hope again. You will conquer depression.

## LIFEFILTER #29

Today, I will:

- Remember: God can use even my depression for His glory.

- Stop right now and thank God for His incredible love!

Scripture To Strengthen Me:

"But he said to me, 'My grace is sufficient for you, for my power is made perfect in weakness.' Therefore I will boast all the more gladly about my weaknesses, so that Christ's power may rest on me." 2 Corinthians 12:9

# 30

# DAY THIRTY

# THE POWER TO CONQUER

Congratulations! You've made it to the last chapter; the last day! But where do you go from here?

A more correct question would be: Where do *we* go from here? If you flip back to the beginning of the book, you'll find our promise to help you put together a team that will stay with you for the rest of your life. So, if you don't mind, we'd like to continue to be a part of your everyday life.

How can we do this? The following are some suggestions and hints to help you continue discovering joy and conquering depression:

- **Read the book again!** Did you absorb and master every concept of every chapter? You don't have to spend as much time on every chapter as before, but I guarantee reading *HOPE AGAIN: A 30-Day Plan for Conquering Depression* a second time will help you discover things in the book you missed the first time.
- **Recommend the book to a friend who might need it.** Am I suggesting this so we can sell another copy? Sure! No, the truth is that Bruce and I believe deeply

in God's power to use this book in the lives of those who are depressed. But the overall reason I want you to share knowledge of this book with someone else is that it will give you something positive to discuss with a friend. And in talking about your depression, you begin to lessen its power. In listening to the problems of your friend, you may be able to help them out of the dark pit that overwhelms them.

- **Continue to use your LifeFilters.** Carry one of them with you every day for the foreseeable future, or look at them every day. Perhaps three or four of them touch especially sensitive areas of your life. If so, you might want to keep one of these, in addition to the regular rotation of **LifeFilters**, always with you.
- **Read your Bible every day.** It is absolutely imperative that you feed yourself spiritually every day. The health of your soul depends upon your doing this.
- **Pray without ceasing.** Actually, the apostle Paul said this a long time before I thought of it. But the advice is still good. I have gotten in the habit of lifting what I call "little prayers" up to God forty or fifty times a day. On the way to work, I pray for every member of my family. In the first minutes of getting to my office, I ask God for His wisdom and protection through the day. And about once an hour, I thank God for His love. I think Paul knew this kind of attitude keeps us focused upon God, even while living in and dealing with this world.
- **Attend church regularly.** Don't let anything or anyone drive you away from your church. Don't let any emotion have control over your church attendance. If you haven't yet done so, find a church

where the Bible is accepted as authoritative for all aspects of life, and where the pastor applies it to *your* life.
- **Follow the doctor's instructions (see below).** Bruce has some wonderful prescriptions in the next section for overcoming depression. Follow them faithfully!
- **Know that I am praying for you *every day*.** If you are holding this book and reading these words, then I am praying for you. In fact, I have prayed for you every day as I've written this book. Before you ever picked it up, I prayed that God would lead you to find this book and read it. As you've gone through the chapters, I've prayed God would give you the strength to follow these instructions and conquer depression. And now that you've finished the book, know that neither God nor I am finished with you. He will always love you and be there for you. I have covenanted with God to pray every day for you.
- **Write to me.** If this book has blessed you, or if you have a special prayer request, I invite you to email me at mwrites@bellsouth.net. I don't guarantee I can answer every email personally, but I do promise to read every letter and pray for every need.

Let me close with a story about you.

Many years ago in India, a water carrier trudged from his home to the river every day. There he would fill two huge clay pots with water and then put them on his shoulders, a stout pole holding them in place. He would then return to his home and use the water in his daily tasks.

One of the pots was always sad during the return trip. This is because small fissures ran across its surface, allowing water to leak out. By the time its master had gotten to his home, fully half of the pot's water was gone. Because it loved the master, this pot felt guilty for being such a poor container.

One day the pot got up enough courage to speak to its master. "Oh sir," it said, "I am so sorry to cause you so much trouble."

"What are you talking about?" asked the master.

The pot was ashamed. "Because I am such a poor container, I waste the precious water you gather. The cracks in my surface make me unworthy to help you any more. I wish to be thrown away."

Smiling gently, the master said, "You have completely misunderstood. There are other pots without cracks I could be using. You have seen them by the side of the house. Haven't you ever wondered why I insist on using you instead of them?"

The pot had to admit it had often wondered this very thing.

"It's because you can do something for me none of the others can do."

"Me?" The clay pot was incredulous. "I have cracks and fissures that make me weak. How is this possible?"

"I am the master," the man replied. "I see and plan things you do not begin to understand. But this once, I will show you how you are uniquely valuable to me." And picking up the cracked clay pot, he began walking toward the river.

"Do you see how beautiful the flowers are on this road?"

The pot nodded with wonder. It had never really noticed the beauty evident on the journey to and from the river. Instead, it had always focused on its weaknesses.

"After filling you each day, I always make sure to put you on the shoulder closest to the side of the road. As I walk, your cracks and fissures allow the water to trickle out and nourish the soil between the river and our home. As a result, this portion of the land is more beautiful than any other."

The pot was stunned. "Do you mean to say I have had a part in bringing about this beauty?"

The master nodded. "It is *only* because of your system of cracks and fissures that these flowers have been able to bloom. Your weaknesses, given to me, have become your strengths. Through them, together we have created wondrous beauty."

You, fellow struggler, are the cracked clay pot. A vessel lined with cracks and fissures. Perhaps you feel your depression makes you a poor container for God's love.

**Focus upon your weaknesses, and you'll never see the beauty in life's journey.**

Place too much guilt upon yourself, and you'll never notice how God wants to use you.

But if you will give your depression to God and allow Him to use you – weaknesses and all – then He will begin to show how His strength is made perfect in your weakness. He'll draw your attention to the lives touched by your compassion and sensitivity.

**Your Heavenly Father, who loves you so deeply He allowed His only Son to die for you, will take your weaknesses and, out of them, create works of wondrous beauty.**

Realize that your depression just might be the best tool God has to do some great things and touch some needy lives. Thank Him for using you for His glory. And, one more thing. Look up and enjoy the journey.

*"Keep yourselves in God's love as you wait for the mercy of our Lord Jesus Christ to bring you to eternal life. Be merciful to those who doubt. [And now], to him who is able to keep you from falling and to present you before his glorious presence without fault and with great joy— to the only God*

*our Savior be glory, majesty, power and authority, through Jesus Christ our Lord, before all ages, now and forevermore! Amen." (Jude 21-22, 24-25)*

Blessings,
Mark

# KNOWLEDGE IS POWER

"Open the glove box and look inside." Jimmy's eyes were filling with tears. His hands were so tightly gripped on the steering wheel, his arms were shaking. I pressed the glove box latch, and the lid fell down into my lap. There nestled against aging papers and discarded candy wrappers lay a gun, beetle black and shining. My mouth grew dry, and my heart accelerated. I looked through the windshield at the weed-filled yard of the house Jimmy had parked in front of.

"What is this for?" I whispered.

"If I had not found you today, I was going to come here where I used to live and kill myself."

The air grew still, and I blinked in shock and surprise. Jimmy and his family had moved back to their hometown over a year ago, and I had not heard from him. Until today. He had driven from his hometown an hour away and had appeared in my driveway.

"Why, Jimmy?" Was all I could manage.

"We moved back to our hometown. It was a dream come true that turned into a nightmare. She left me for an old flame."

Tears were streaming down his face. "Why would God do this to me?"

I swallowed and tried to find words. I closed the glove box door. "Jimmy, you can't do this. Who would take care of your kids? You can't abandon them to their mother after she left them." *God help me*, I prayed. "You are the only stable force in their lives right now. You don't have the option of taking the easy way out." I studied Jimmy's old house and the weed-choked yard. "This is the past, Jimmy. It's gone. You can't change that now. But, your kids need you. Let's go. Now. Get out of here. Leave this behind."

Jimmy stiffly threw the car in gear. He drove aimlessly, and I suggested we go to the riverfront for our city's fall festival, Red River Revel. Once there, Jimmy followed me away from his car; away from the gun. We wandered through booths filled with art and filled with crafts that moved and flapped in the cool afternoon air. I watched his attention drawn to the kids who laughed and ran around their parents. We sampled regional food, and slowly, Jimmy seemed to begin to come back to life. He began to breathe again.

A shadow fell over us. We had wandered beneath the Texas Street bridge, an ancient span that took travelers from downtown Shreveport across the swirling waters of Red River into our sister city, Bossier City. People were gathered around one of the huge support beams of the bridge. As I neared, I noticed that an artist had drawn a sprawling bayou scene on the old concrete. People busily sifted through broken tiles in buckets and, after dabbing grout on the tile, pressed pieces into the outlines of the picture. Slowly, the huge tapestry came to life with color and life.

"Let's do something constructive," I told Jimmy. He nodded, and we took our place before a blank section of the support beam. As the cool afternoon waned, we tirelessly picked through buckets of broken tile, searching for the right colors to match the scene before us. Jimmy filled in the outlines of two frogs. I brought a turtle to life. Suddenly, I realized my bucket was empty. I was out of green.

I took the empty bucket and noticed a table nearby. Behind the table, the Artist stood. His chest was covered with a leather apron, and a carpenter's belt surrounded his waist. He wiped sweat from his brow with gloved hands and handed a bucket to an eager woman.

He reached beneath the table and lifted a heavy cardboard box. His muscles bulged, and the veins stood out on his neck as the box thudded onto the table. His gloved hands tore the box open, and he dumped the contents onto the table. Perfectly formed tiles spilled out into the autumn sunshine. They glittered with their pristine glazed finish. Each tile formed a flawless square. Their colors reflected in the Artist's eyes as he reached to his carpenter's belt. From there, he withdrew a mallet hammer, scarred and dull. The arms of his muscles bulged as he lifted the hammer above his head. His face grew solemn in concentration, and I gasped as I realized his intent. The hammer descended with a thunderous din amidst the perfect tiles. The tiles shattered beneath the impact of the hammer, bits, and pieces showering around the Artist. One piece of tile caught the Artist on the forehead, and a line of crimson appeared. Breaking the tiles was costly!

I wanted to scream. I wanted to shout. I wanted to dive over the tiles; to stop the terrible descent of the hammer as the Artist broke the tiles again and again. They were perfect! They were just the right shape! Why would he break them? Why?

Tears clouded my vision as the Artist finished his demolition. He placed the hammer back in his belt and wiped the blood from his brow. His mighty hands swept the broken bits of tile into a bucket, and he placed the bucket on the table before me. His eyes burned into mine.

"Why?" was all I could manage.

"I can't use the tile unless it is broken." He said. I took the bucket in numb hands and felt dizzy. I backed away and bumped into Jimmy. I turned and looked into his shocked eyes.

"He had to break the tiles. He had to break the tiles." Jimmy said hoarsely.

"Yes. We made them perfect. We made them square and seamless and shiny. But, He can't use them unless they're imperfect." I said.

Jimmy grabbed me and pulled me into a tight embrace. The bucket fell to the ground, pieces of shattered tile spilling around our feet. We cried together for what seemed like an eternity. Jimmy pushed away, and there was life in his eyes. He smiled. "He had to break the tiles, Bruce. He had to break them."

"Our tiles," I said. I was grinning from ear to ear. "Jimmy, just imagine the tapestry that waits. Imagine what it will look like when He is done."

Jimmy scooped the broken bits of tile from the ground, and we turned again to the mural on the bridge. We finished our section and stepped back. The frogs were embracing in love. The turtle was gazing at the sun setting on the bayou. Rough concrete and scrawled lines and broken tile had become a masterpiece.

Jimmy went on to raise his children and married again. He started a film ministry and became active in church work. He changed lives. He made the world a better place. He picked up the broken pieces of his life and handed them to the Artist.

We have come to the end of this book. We have completed a 30 day journey through knowledge and pain and scripture and, hopefully, encouragement. We have journeyed from despair to hope. Mark and I have both been broken; shattered by the hands of God; by the hammer of circumstances; by the sledgehammer of life.

**But, there is one thing God has shown us. Only when we are broken can He use us.**

Only when we have dropped the "perfect" tiles of the life we have tried to build can they shatter. The night I descended into my deep, dark depression, I was broken, shattered, splintered, and stripped of everything I had built.

God scooped up my broken pieces and put them in His bucket. He handed them to the Artist, His Son, my Redeemer, and my One true love. There, under the careful hand of the Son of God, I was rebuilt; reshaped; transformed into a tapestry that is wondrous and beautiful to my Master. It is not the mural that I would have painted. It is not the art that I would have created. But, it is the life, the Story that God intended. It is the story we have shared in this book.

You see, *the* story is part of the redemption. *Your* story is part of the redemption, and the ending is yet to come! What wondrous things will the Artist do through you?

**Who is waiting on the other side of your brokenness to be encouraged; aided; loved by the journey you are walking? If you walk with God, then the story will have a wondrous ending. And, the sequel will be breathtaking!**

You have been broken. You have descended into the valley of the shadow of death. But, it is only a shadow. And, God has promised to lift you up; to take your broken life and rebuild it. Let the depression that broke you, that shattered you, be the force that drives you to pick up the pieces and hand them to God.

The Artist desires your life and your love, and only when your hands are empty can He rebuild your life. Give Him your broken, imperfect life today, and the Artist, the Creator of the universe will make a tapestry of your life unequaled by any human artist; a picture of eternity!

Blessings,

Bruce Hennigan

## LIFEFILTER #30

Today, I will:

- Give my broken life to God and allow Him to use the pieces to make me a part of His picture of eternity.

- Start over with **LifeFilter** #1 tomorrow!

Scripture To Strengthen Me:

*"To him who is able to keep you from stumbling and to present you before his glorious presence without fault and with great joy—to the only God our Savior be glory, majesty, power and authority, through Jesus Christ our Lord, before all ages, now and forevermore! Amen." Jude 24–25*

# ENDNOTES

[1] Mark S. Gold, M.D., *The Good News About Depression*, pg. 170, New York, NY, © 1995.

[2] Charles Stanley, *How to Handle Adversity*, Oliver-Nelson Books, Nashville, TN, © 1989, page 101.

[3] Proclaim: The Magazine of Preaching; October-December, 1992.

[4] Editor's Clip Sheets, Logos Productions Inc., South St. Paul, MN, December, 1993, page 3.

[5] Alice Grey, *Stories for the Heart*, Multnomah Books, Sisters, OR, © 1996, pg. 88.

[6] Barbara Johnson, *Mama, Get the Hammer, There's a Fly on Papa's Head!*, Word Publishing, Dallas, © 1994, pg 95.

[7] Carol Hart, *Secrets of Serotonin*, St. Martin's Press, Boston, © 1996, pg. 25.

[8] Lucy Jo Palladin, *Find Your Focus Zone: An Effective Plan to Defeat Distraction and Overload*, Simon and Schuster Digital Sales, Inc., 2007

[9] Charles Duhigg, *The Power of Habit: Why We Do What We Do in Life and Business*, Random House 2012

[10] Medard Laz, *Love Adds A Little Chocolate*, Warner Books, New York, NY, © 1997, pg. 85..

[11] *Homiletics*, May, 1998, pg.36.

[12] John L. Mason, *An Enemy Called Average*, © 1990, pg.49.

[13] Harbaugh WT, Mayr U, Burghart DR. Neural Responses to Taxation and Voluntary Giving Reveal Motives for Charitable Donations. *Science*, June 2007.

[14] Katherine Zeratsy, R. D., L. D.,Mayo Clinic, http://www.mayoclinic.com/health/depression-and-diet/AN02057

[15] Akbaraly TN, et al. Dietary pattern and depressive symptoms in middle age. British Journal of Psychiatry. 2009; pgs 195-408.

[16] John C. Maxwell, *The Success Journey*, Thomas Nelson Publishers, Nashville, TN, © 1997, pgs.155-156.

[17] The Creative Life: A Workbook for Unearthing the Christian Imagination by Alice Bass, InterVarsity Press, 2001.

[18] http://www.webmd.com/mental-health/news/20021205/unraveling-suns-role-in-depression

[19] "Chronic pain and depression: Twin burdens of adaptation". Christina M. Van Puymbroeck, Ph.D., Alex J. Zautra, Ph.D.,

& Peter-Panagioti Harakas, MS. Department of Psychology Arizona State University

P.O. Box 871104

Tempe, Arizona 85287-1104. In A. Steptoe (Ed.) *Depression and Chronic Illness*. Cambridge: Cambridge University Press, in press.

[20] Billy Graham, *Unto the Hills*, Word Publishing, Dallas, TX, © 1996, pg. 53.

[21] Hooked on Games: The Lure and Cost of Video Game and Internet Addiction by Andrew Doan, Ph. D., M.D. FEP International, August 2012.

[22] The Demise of Guys: Why Boys Are Struggling and What

We Can Do About It by Phillip Zimbardo and Nikita Duncan, TED Conferences, May, 2012.
[23] ibid.

# ADDITIONAL RESOURCES

Sean McDowell, "So the Next Generation Will Know (New York: David Cook - TBG), 2019. This is an excellent book for anyone wishing to understand the "Digital Generation" that is our teenagers and pre-teens as of 2019.

C. S. Lewis, "The C. S. Lewis Signature Classics (8-Volume Box Set): An Anthology of 8 C. S. Lewis Titles: Mere Christianity, The Screwtape Letters, Miracles, The ... The Abolition of Man, and The Four Loves", (New York, Harper One), 2017

"Understanding Depression" from Harvard Medical School is an excellent summary of the newest medical information on depression and can be found at https://www.health.harvard.edu/mind-and-mood/understanding-depression

J. P. Moreland's lecture on TRUTH can be seen at https://www.youtube.com/watch?v=ayWunD3ECPY and go ahead and check out all the lectures from the AMP Conferences.

# THE AUTHORS

Mark Sutton

Mark Sutton, founder of Mark Sutton Ministries, has worked as a full time minister for more than 40 years. He and his wife, Donna, have 5 children and currently live in central Florida, where Mark teaches pastors and church leaders, both in Florida and in Haiti. Mark is the author of 5 books, more than 200 articles, and is currently putting the finishing touches on 2 Christian novels.

For more information on Mark's Haiti minister go to marksuttonministries.org.

Bruce Hennigan

*PROFILE*

Bruce Hennigan was born in Blanchard, Louisiana and moved to Shreveport to attend medical school. He is currently in the practice of radiology with the Willis Knighton Health Care System. He is also a published author, a Christian apologist, a dramatist, and a public speaker.

Bruce joined Brookwood Baptist Church in 1975. He married Sherry Kidd in 1980 and together, they have been faithful members since that time. They have two grown children, Sean Hennigan (and his wife Dr. Jennifer Attaway Hennigan) of Abilene, Texas and Casey Hennigan of Shreveport,

Louisiana. Bruce was ordained as a deacon by Brookwood Baptist Church in 1985. Bruce served in multiple leadership capacities at Brookwood Baptist Church as well as teaching small groups for years, particularly in the field of Christian apologetics. He is currently a trustee of Brookwood Baptist Church.

*EXPERIENCE*

**APOLOGETICS:**

Volunteer apologist with Reasons to Believe 1999-present.

An apologist is one who defends the truthfulness of the Christian faith through evidence from science, history and philosophy. Bruce completed a two year training program with the organization, Reasons to Believe (reasons.org).

Certified Apologetic Instructor 2008-present

Bruce completed a three year program with the Apologetic division of the North American Mission Board of the Southern Baptist Convention as well as receiving a Certificate of Apologetics from BIOLA University. This project was under the direction of Mike Licona (risenjesus.org).

Bruce teaches apologetics with his teaching partner, Mark Riser (markriserapologist.com)

**DRAMA:**

Drama director at Brookwood Baptist Church 1992-2006

Bruce was the director of the drama ministry at Brookwood Baptist Church from 1992 to 2006 and in that capacity oversaw a ministry with, at times, over 150 participants. He produced, directed, wrote, and acted in many of the productions during this time. Bruce has written over 100 short and long dramas and is a frequent speaker at regional drama festivals on play writing, directing, organizing a drama ministry, just to name a few topics.

Creative Director of Kidstuf, (a family/children's worship experience) at Brookwood Baptist Church 2010 - 2015

**AUTHOR:**

Published author 1995-present

Bruce has published several books. His non fiction works are two books on depression and a collection of children's dramas. His fiction books are supernatural thrillers about spiritual warfare. His latest books center around spiritual issues of the past, particularly at the beginning of WWII.

**The Chronicles of Jonathan Steel**

The 13th Demon: Altar of the Spiral Eye (Realms Books) 2011

The 12th Demon: Mark of the Wolf Dragon (Realms Books) 2012

The 11th Demon: The Ark of Chaos (Westbow Press), 2013

The 10th Demon: Children of the Bloodstone (Area 613 imprint, 613media, LLC.), 2015

Death by Darwin (a prequel to the 13th Demon), (Area 613, 613media, LLC.), 2017

The 9th Demon: Time of the Cross (Area 613), 2018

More information on "The Chronicles of Jonathan Steel" can be found at steelchronicles.com and brucehennigan.com.

**Standing Tall Books:**

The Homecoming Tree (Standing Tall Books, 613media, LLC.), 2018

More information on these inspirational books can be found at homecomingtree.com and brucehennigan.com.

**The Depression Series:**

Conquering Depression, B&H Publishing, 2001

Hope Again: A 30 Day Plan for Conquering Depression, B&H Publishing, 2014

Hope Again: A Lifetime Plan for Conquering Depression, Hope Again Books, an imprint of LifeFilters, LLC. 2019

For more information on these books and our Conquering Depression Seminar, go to conqueringdepression.com.

**Future Books:**

The 8th Demon: A Wicked Numinosity

The Node of God: The Day of the Harbinger (Book 1)

The 5 Minute Atheist

What is the Lie? — Dismantling the Lies of Culture with Mark Sutton

www.ingramcontent.com/pod-product-compliance
Lightning Source LLC
Chambersburg PA
CBHW070418010526
44118CB00014B/1809